AMBIGUOUS LEGACY

AMBIGUOUS LEGACY

THE LEFT IN AMERICAN POLITICS

JAMES WEINSTEIN

New Viewpoints
A Division of Franklin Watts, Inc.
New York 1975

Library of Congress Cataloging in Publication Data

Weinstein, James, 1926–
    Ambiguous legacy.

    Includes bibliographical references and index.
    1. Socialism in the United States. 2. Communism—
United States—1917–   3. Radicalism—United States.
4. United States—Politics and government—20th century.
I. Title.
HX89.W43   320.9'73'09   75-1189
ISBN 0-531-05368-7
ISBN 0-531-05575-2 pbk.

Manufactured in the United States of America
6 5 4 3 2 1

Contents

Preface

The American left since 1900 has started anew and failed three times. Each time the organized movement has had illusions of a revolutionary destiny, but each movement has been relatively short-lived. The collapse of each attempt, in part, has been the result of political repression; the more important factor, however, has been political weakness. Each new left, reflecting the dominant empiricism of American capitalist society, has taken its character largely in response to immediate events and has been blind to the larger and more long-term developments of American capitalism and to the historical experience of the socialist left. Because of this, and in the absence of a continuing organized movement with a cumulative experience and theory, the left has been forced to relive the experiences of its predecessors time and time again.

Although their shadows linger on in the form of sectarian parties and groups, these three movements—the old Socialist Party of 1900 to 1919, the Communist Party, which arose after the formation of the Third International in 1919 and finally collapsed in 1956, and the "new left" of the 1960s—have come and gone. In their wake is a continuing need for a socialist left in the United States and a steadily growing potential base for a popular revolutionary movement. At the present time there are several groups on the left attempting to create—or re-create—an organized socialist movement in the United States. Whether any organization now in existence has the possibility of serving as the basis for a popular socialist movement remains to be seen. But without knowledge of its roots, of the achievements and shortcomings of the earlier parties and organizations, a new movement will have no more chance of success than did its predecessors.

Both the Communists and the new leftists of the 1960s thought of themselves as sharply different from their predecessors. In some ways, of course, they were right. The new left in particular never developed a coherent socialist politics. Yet the underlying ideas of all three movements have in many respects been similar. All three (in varying degree) have accepted the syndicalist belief that fighting for immediate interests, for reforms—either in the workplace or in the community—would in itself lead people to a broader understanding of the need for a comprehensive revolutionary movement. The idea that ultimate aims were not at issue and that the immediate movement for reform was all important dominated the popular politics of the Communists since the 1930s and the new left until 1969 when it went off in a frenzy of guilt and despair. The relegation of the need for a socialist revolution to the back rooms of party headquarters and the private lives of movement organizers was first advanced in the socialist movement by Eduard Bernstein and has been reinforced by academic pluralist theory. The widespread, although unconscious, acceptance of these ideas within the left has made it easier for class-conscious capitalists in the United States to retain the initiative and to outmaneuver and defeat each successive socialist (or ''radical'') movement, although in each case other factors have also been important.

Both the Communist movement and the ''new'' left have failed to base their politics on the changing nature of advanced corporate capitalism in the United States. Instead, the various parties and movements have either been radical expressions of interest-group politics or sectarian attempts to duplicate revolutionary movements in preindustrial nations like Russia, China, and Cuba. In this realm of politics the old and new lefts look very much alike despite many other differences.

Yet the old Socialist Party and the new left both had the potential of building a sustained mass movement for socialism in the United States, and that potential still exists in the largely unorganized movement that survives the new left. Unfortunately, the old ideas and concepts of revolutionary politics also survive, which is why this essay has been written. As long as we do not understand why the politics of earlier movements are inappropriate to the changing social relations of advanced capitalism in the United States, we will be condemned to play out variations on earlier themes. The less we know about our history the less we will be able to transcend it.

Capitalism as a social system organizes all human activity—"economic," "political," and "social"—around the need of the capitalist class to create and realize surplus value, around commodity production for profit. This does not mean, of course, that all social institutions are immediately controlled by the large corporations or by greedy individual capitalists. Some institutions—the family, child care, schools, religion, politics—have independence, in varying degrees, in their everyday functioning. But as long as capitalism prevails, none of these institutions—or any others—can develop and permanently put into practice principles that undermine capitalist values and social relations.

A socialist revolution requires, and makes possible, a change in the basic principles that now determine and shape all social decision-making. In American capitalist society the vast majority of people waste their lives in order to make enough money to survive. The nature and purpose of work is not determined by social needs or by the need for creative self-development, but by capital's need to expand and remain profitable. In contrast, the basic principle of socialism is the full and free development of every individual in a community where she or he is an active participant and to which she or he is responsible. Such a society is possible only if power over the political economy is taken from the capitalist class by those who now work for the corporations and the government—either in factories, offices, or schools—in alliance with other social groups—the permanently unemployed, housewives, petty business people—whose needs are not met and whose development is thwarted by the existing social system.

A revolutionary movement embodies the potential for developing social relations on a new basis if it challenges the power of the capitalist class (which now subordinates human needs to the imperatives of commodity production) and if it organizes working people to take power over society as a whole. Only by taking control of the existing state apparatus—the government—can the working class redefine and reorganize production on the basis of democratically determined need. If a socialist movement succeeds, the disguised rule of the few who now own and control productive property will become the popular activity of everyone.

To make a revolution of this kind, the working class must be conscious of itself as a class and must understand its historical potential. If working people are collectively to determine social priorities—if they hope to govern themselves and shape the course of events (make history)—they must understand that capitalism is a hierarchical class system and they must understand and want socialism, a system in which there is no subordinate working class, no systematically oppressed classes or groups. And, of course, they must join together in a popular movement to take power from the capitalist class and attain socialism. In short, a socialist movement (led by a party) must consciously and openly seek to transform capitalist society as a whole.

Although the organized left in the United States is currently weak and nearly invisible, the American socialist movement has had a long and, in some ways, a rich history. This brief essay examines that history from the emergence of the Socialist Party of America in 1901—the coming of age of American socialism—to the disintegration of the new left in the late 1960s. Of necessity, I have excluded many aspects of this history; but I have tried to trace the central developments of the Socialist, Communist, and new left movements, and to explore their major strengths and weaknesses. I do so as a socialist involved in and concerned with the creation of a new socialist party in the United States—one that can build upon the experiences of the American left in this century.

Clifford Solway suggested that I write this book, and although it has in many ways been painful work, I am grateful to him for doing so. He and others who read and criticized all or portions of the manuscript persuaded me to revise major sections of the original draft. I am most deeply indebted to Al Richmond and John Judis for their careful readings and vigorous criticisms. Although Richmond does not share my overall estimate of the Communist Party's role when it was the hegemonic force on the American left, he nevertheless made many useful suggestions and corrected several substantial errors. Likewise, Judis's criticism prompted a revision of the entire section on the Socialist Party and he made many other valuable suggestions.

In addition, Dorothy Healey, Barbara Easton, and Bruce Dancis read various drafts, made suggestions for changes, and registered disagreements. These, too, have been helpful, if not always followed. It is customary at this point for the author to accept sole responsibility for the defects of his or her work. Modesty prevents me from doing so. I am, of course, at least partly responsible for the faults and weaknesses of this book, but like its virtues, the book's shortcomings are as much a reflection of the collective experiences of active socialists over the last three-quarters of a century as they are my own.

San Francisco, California
May 1974

1/

THE SOCIALIST PARTY OF AMERICA

Background

The years from 1897 to 1904—during which the Socialist Party of America was organized—were the period of the most decisive series of mergers and consolidations in American industrial history. In these eight years, corporations with assets of $6 billion were organized, compared with about $1 billion in corporate mergers in the previous eighteen years. By 1904 the top 4 percent of American concerns (the great majority of which were corporate in form) produced 57 percent of the total industrial output by value. By any standard of measurement, large corporations had come to dominate the American economy, and the form of competition known in the nineteenth century was doomed. In conjunction with these changes in economic organization, corporate leaders began to abandon laissez-faire liberalism (the idea of free competition and the less government interference the better—except to protect business from attack by workers).

From 1850 to 1900, as industrialization swept the United States, the process of capital accumulation brought with it a steady, relative, and absolute increase in the industrial work force, a spontaneous opposition to their working conditions and low wages by the newly proletarianized workers, and many bitter, violent strikes and insurrections.

The depth of this spontaneous anti-capitalist sentiment among the farm boys, artisans, and others entering the rapidly expanding industrial work force was demonstrated during the great railroad strikes of 1877 when tens of thousands of railroad and factory workers poured out of their shops to attack company property, the police, and anyone else or thing that threatened to stifle the expression of their anger. In Pittsburgh, where almost the entire city supported the workers, 104 locomotives, 2,154 railroad cars, and roundhouses, sheds, the depot, offices, and other railroad property were burned to the ground, along with the city's grain elevator and other buildings. When the elevator was under attack, an official of the elevator company argued that it was not railroad property and should be spared. But a striker yelled: "It's owned by a damned monopoly—let it burn." And it did. The Pittsburgh *Leader* quoted a striker as saying, even if "so-called law and order" should beat them down, "we would at least have our revenge on the men who have coined our sweat and blood into millions for themselves," while leaving the workers to starve. And a militiaman reported that he could find but a single spirit among the strikers: "that they were justified in resorting to any means to break the power of the corporations." [1]

During this period of explosive, chaotic development, the granting of wage increases or other ameliorative improvements was usually understood by individual entrepreneurs and small corporations as a threat to their competitive positions and, therefore, to their continued existence as capitalist enterprises. In this situation a wage increase could not be overcome by a price increase unless all competing companies in a given industry simultaneously granted the same increase—which was virtually impossible given the large number of widely scattered competitors. Increases in wages could only come out of profits. That meant a slower rate of expansion and therefore a competitive disadvantage and possible bankruptcy. No wonder then that employers viewed unions as threats to their class position and resisted unionization so fiercely. And no wonder that radicals and revolutionaries saw the fight for union recognition and contractual agreements as inherently revolutionary.

Such struggles, broadened and exacerbated by periodic economic

[1] See Robert V. Bruce, *1877, Year of Violence* (Chicago, 1970), pp. 180, 176, 136, 182.

crises, were expected to lead to revolution. Instead, they led to liberal corporate capitalism. The process of change was prolonged and not readily apparent, even with hindsight, until the reforms of the Progressive Era (1900–1917). But even by the time of the Haymarket riots in 1886, the early, spontaneous anti-corporatism was coming under control, and the large corporations and conditions of quasi-monopoly, on which the political economy of corporate liberalism would be based, were developing. With the rise of the large corporation, and particularly after the merger movement of 1897–1904, the meaning of trade unionism, at least to the larger manufacturers, began to change. By the early 1900s several basic industries were beginning to eliminate price competition by agreement among themselves (as in the famous "Gary dinners" in the steel industry, at which Elbert H. Gary of United States Steel would announce the price of steel to be charged by his company, thereby setting prices for the industry for the coming year) or through federal regulation of rates, as in the railroad industry. In these industries wage increases, either as a result of union organization or as a means of keeping the union out, were passed on to the consumer.

The persistence of nineteenth-century attitudes among businessmen, workers, and farmers—and among Socialists themselves—as well as the persistence of many of the social conditions of the competitive period of industrialization, provided the basis for the rapid growth of the Socialist Party in the very years that its specific analysis of capitalism was becoming archaic. The Socialist Party was formed when the large corporations were just beginning to change their attitudes toward non-revolutionary unions and toward social reform. For the most part, trade union struggles remained fierce during the Progressive Era, and the harsh realities of social life required militant struggles for social reform. Understood within the theoretical model of competitive capitalism, these struggles were expected by Socialists to create a mass revolutionary movement. And, for several years, they did.

By the same token, the growth of the socialist movement forced capitalists to move toward humanizing large-scale industrial production. Fierce trade union struggles had gone on for decades. Ironically, these struggles finally led to the emergence of a unified socialist movement just as the more sophisticated corporations were beginning to organize to reduce overt class antagonism and the threat of class-conscious politics that a frustrated trade union movement was producing. Within this political context, the challenge presented by a growing socialist movement helped shape the development of corporate liberalism during the Progressive Era of 1900–1917. But precisely because the development of corporate liberalism was in large part a response to the long-term struggles in which the Socialists participated, it was difficult for them to understand the changes in the political economy then taking place.

Socialism and Syndicalism

In the United States many parties and groups have considered themselves socialist or revolutionary, but none has come close to building a movement capable of taking state power. Of these parties and groups, the old Socialist Party of America (1901–1919) came closest to this goal in that it built a popular movement infused with the intention of transforming the United States from a capitalist society to a socialist democracy. The party's potential lay in its commitment to democracy and in its strategy of making socialism vs. capitalism a central question in all of its public activity. By making millions of people aware of capitalism as a class system run by capitalists in their own interests, and by convicing these millions that socialism was necessary for the development of their full human potential—and that the party intended to take power and establish a socialist society—the old Socialist Party established the basis for a genuinely revolutionary movement. The Socialists made millions of people think about making their own history. Although it concentrated on immediate conditions, the party also lifted people above the narrow concerns of daily life in which people under capitalism are normally encased: how to survive, how to gain a measure of material comfort and security, or—at best—how to advance their own careers or solve their personal problems within the existing system of social relations.

But the Socialist Party also had one of the basic failings that later facilitated the Communist Party's adoption of reformist politics and its absorption by large-scale corporate capitalism during the New Deal. Stated most generally, the Socialist Party's failing was its historical determinism, its belief that the capitalist class would not be able to adjust to—or survive—the contradictions of competitive capitalism, and that consequently the struggles of working people to reform capitalism would simply deepen the contradictions of capitalist society and precipitate a final crisis. American Socialists, like European Social Democrats, believed that they would necessarily be the political beneficiaries of reforms, and they expected gradually to accumulate a larger and larger following until they were voted into power, aided, of necessity, by a highly organized trade union movement.

Almost all Socialists saw the unions as the economic arm of the working class and the party as its political arm. Most believed that industrial unionism (all workers in an industry organized into the same union), as opposed to the craft unionism then prevalent, was a necessary prerequisite to class unity. As Eugene V. Debs argued in 1910, once industrial unionism was achieved, "economic unity will be speedily followed by political unity." The workers, "once united in one great industrial union, will vote a united working class ticket." [2]

The two main centers of Socialist activity were union activity and electoral politics (although the party and its members were active in many other areas). And the relationship between trade unionism and a revolutionary movement was one of the central problems facing Socialists and radicals in the early twentieth century. At their clearest, Socialists saw unions as natural defensive organizations, as the spontaneous creation of workers to defend their immediate interests, while they saw the party as the self-conscious creation of revolutionaries intent on ending the domination of the working class by the capitalist class. The unions functioned to improve conditions within class society. The party was organized not simply to help workers improve their lot as workers, but to destroy capitalism and establish a society in which there would be no distinct class of workers. This view of trade unionism was implicit in the Socialist Party's form of organization, which was aimed at taking control of the state, where capitalists functioned together as a class.

Side by side with this political tendency, revolutionary syndicalism was present in varying degree in the thinking and practice of many Socialists and radical unionists. Revolutionary syndicalists believed that union activity would bring the workers to a revolutionary consciousness as a result of fighting for their own immediate interests. For the syn-

---

[2] Arthur Schlesinger, Jr., ed., *Writings and Speeches of Eugene V. Debs* (New York, 1948), p. 332.

dicalist, the party was either unnecessary, or at best secondary, to the union. Syndicalists envisioned sharper and sharper struggles at the point of production, leading to a general strike (in which the state would be helpless and capitalists would be unable to carry on production) and then to the reorganization of society around the factories.

Both the political and syndicalist tendencies were present within the Socialist Party and also within the Industrial Workers of the World (IWW) and, to a lesser degree, within the American Federation of Labor (AFL). The political tendency was dominant within the party, and the Socialist Party was clearly the major organization on the left from 1901, when it was formally estabished, until 1919, when the Communist and Communist Labor parties were formed. After 1919, various political tendencies on the left generally formed separate parties or groups. Before 1919 almost all existed as tendencies within the Socialist Party, which itself represented the strength and diversity of the popular movement for socialism in the United States.

/ Socialism Before the Great War

When the Socialist Party came together in 1901 it was still an uneasy amalgam of earlier parties and groups. The largest of the coalescing groups was the Social Democracy of America, which, in turn, was made up of the German Social Democrats of Milwaukee (led by Victor Berger) and the remnants of his American Railway Union (led by Eugene V. Debs), which had been destroyed by the government in the Pullman strike of 1894. Next most important was a group of former Socialist Labor Party members who had broken with Daniel De Leon because of his insistence on building the Socialist Trade and Labor Alliance as a dual union in opposition to the AFL. This group included Morris Hillquit of New York and several leading trade unionists, such as Max Hayes of the Typographical union in Cleveland and J. Mahlon Barnes of the Philadelphia Cigar Makers. The Social Democrats and former Socialist Laborites were mostly from the East and Midwest and were predominantly trade unionists working within the AFL. They were joined by two other major groups, former populists, mostly from Oklahoma, Texas, and other southwestern states, and the Christian Socialists, many of whom had been followers of Edward Bellamy in the 1880s and '90s.

In his first campaign for the presidency, Eugene Debs polled almost 100,000 votes, an all-time high for a Socialist candidate up to that time. A few months later, when the party was officially organized, it had almost 10,000 members. In the next dozen years, the Socialists increased their membership by more than tenfold and their vote by almost that amount. In 1912 Debs polled 901,000 votes (6 percent of the total), and the party had 120,000 members paying dues each month. Socialist strength by then was considerable. More than 340 cities and towns had elected some 1,200 party members to public office. Socialists published more than 300 daily, weekly, and monthly publications, one of which, *The Appeal to Reason,* would soon reach a circulation of 761,000 per week. Within the AFL, Socialists controlled several important unions—the Machinists, the Western Federation of Miners, the Brewery Workers—and had a substantial influence in others, most notably the United Mine Workers of America. Socialists led the state federations of labor in Pennsylvania, Illinois, Wisconsin, and Missouri.

Until the United States entered World War I in 1917, the Socialist Party was diffuse geographically. The party's greatest relative voting strength, for example, was west of the Mississippi River, in the states where mining, lumbering, or tenant farming prevailed. The states with the highest percentage of Socialist votes in the prewar years were Oklahoma, Nevada, Montana, Washington, California, Idaho, Florida, Arizona, Wisconsin, and Texas, in that order. All were among the top dozen states in the presidential elections in 1912 and 1916. Oklahoma had the most complete organization: 12,000 party members in 961 locals, 38,000 subscribers to *The Appeal to Reason,* and 53,000 voters. In 1914, five Socialists were elected to the Oklahoma Assembly, one to the State Senate, and more than 130 held county or township offices.

The party experienced its most rapid growth before 1912, when it got its highest percentage of the vote in a national election and elected its greatest number of municipal officers (mayors in seventy-three cities and towns, including Milwaukee, Schenectady, and Berkeley). Thereafter, until 1917 when the United States entered World War I, socialism remained a central issue in public life, and the party maintained its overall strength. During these years few social movements were untouched by the question of socialism and the participation of Socialists. The National Association for the Advancement of Colored People

(NAACP), for example, was founded mostly by Socialists (including W. E. B. Du Bois), and party members made up most of the NAACP's leadership in its early years. The first articles on birth control to be widely circulated in the United States were published in the New York *Daily Call,* a Socialist newspaper; the party was an important force in the victory of women's suffrage in California (1911), Kansas (1912), Nevada (1914), and New York (1917); and women were elected to the party's leading bodies and were occasionally party candidates for public office.

But the party's relationship to the unions was of central importance to the growth of socialism, both in the minds of party leaders and in fact. There were two major questions about workplace organizing that Socialists faced in these years: dual unionism, which meant organizing "revolutionary" unions outside of the AFL and often in competition with AFL unions; and revolutionary syndicalism, which was the dominant tendency in the Industrial Workers of the World, but also was the ideology of some radicals in the AFL. Dual unionism and syndicalism were closely related questions. Since syndicalists believed that the workplace was the center of revolutionary politics—and that unions and the experience of struggling around trade union issues were the key organizational activities for revolutionaries—it was difficult for most syndicalists to work within so obviously a conservative federation of unions as the AFL.

The difficulty was increased by the AFL's overall form of organization, which was along craft, rather than industrial, lines. There were some industrial unions in the AFL—that is, unions that admitted into their ranks all those who worked in a given industry, and the Socialists were generally strong in those unions, which included the Brewery Workers, the Western Federation of Miners, the International Ladies Garment Workers, and the United Mine Workers (which had a mixed form of organization). But the majority of AFL unions were organized along occupational lines—carpenters, plumbers, typographers, etc.— and these unions jealously guarded their jurisdictional rights. When, for example, the Brewers tried to include coopers (barrel makers), firemen, engineers, and teamsters working in breweries in their ranks, the various craft unions fought them and in 1907 expelled the Brewers from the AFL (although they were readmitted in 1908).

This firm adherence to craft unionism on the part of the AFL was one of the reasons that Socialists who believed in industrial unionism helped organize the IWW in 1905. At its founding, the IWW included such political Socialists as Debs and A. M. Simons; syndicalists who were party members, such as William D. Haywood, dual unionists from the Socialists Trade and Labor Alliance (led by Daniel De Leon); and many delegates who simply wanted to build industrial unions and who wanted no part of the Socialist Party or any other politics.

The initial dream of the IWW was to organize the mass of unorganized workers in such industries as steel and textiles. In his initial remarks to the founding convention in 1905, Haywood called the gathering a Continental Congress of the working class and declared that the IWW would ''open wide its doors to every man that earns his livelihood either by his brain or his muscle.'' This intention was shared by all present. Debs asserted that the IWW was formed ''for the purpose of uniting the working class'' and would be ''broad enough to embrace every honest worker.'' And Charles O. Sherman, the IWW's first (and only) president, said the IWW would organize not only ''the common man with callous hands'' but also the clerical force, ''the soft hands that only get $40.00 a month, those fellows with the number 10 cuffs and collars.'' [3]

The founders of the IWW did not think they were starting from scratch, but expected that several existing unions might quickly join. The Western Federation of Miners, and its offspring, the American Labor Union, participated in the founding convention. The WFM's 27,000 members made it by far the largest affiliate, but the IWW's expectation that other established unions would join and thus create a coalition of powerful unions was not fulfilled. The Brewery Workers was the first such union expected to quit the AFL and join the IWW, especially since the Brewers had a few delegates at the founding convention. But even after they were expelled from the AFL in 1907, the Brewers did not seriously consider joining the IWW. They needed support from organized workers—especially for the union label on beer and the boycott of non-union beer—and the great majority of organized

[3] Proceedings, the Founding Convention of the IWW (New York, 1969), pp. 1, 143, 586.

workers were in AFL affiliates. Thus they shunned the IWW and entered negotiations to win readmission to the AFL.

The inability to win over the Brewers was indicative of IWW weakness. Part of the difficulty lay in the diversity of political tendencies competing to control the "revolutionary" union. That the two strongest tendencies were anti-political syndicalism and the Socialist Labor Party group did not help. Both were anathema to the Socialist-led WFM as well as to the Brewers. Partly because of the weaknesses of the IWW, symbolized by the Brewers' return to the AFL, and partly because of the developing anti-Socialist Party attitudes, the WFM also lost interest in the IWW and withdrew in 1908.

The loss of the WFM, on top of the failure to win over the Brewers, reduced the IWW to minor importance as a rival to the AFL, particularly in the light of the unrelieved failure of its organizing efforts between 1905 and 1909. In fact, the IWW had been plagued with problems from the beginning. At its second convention, in 1906, the Western Federation of Miners and the Socialists lost control to a group of "anarchists" allied with De Leon. Two years later the "anarchists" ousted De Leon and his followers, who then went off to Detroit and established a rival organization. Meanwhile, the WFM, which had suspended per capita dues payments after the 1906 convention, officially withdrew from the IWW, and Debs quietly dropped his membership.

Debs' brief association with the IWW was motivated by his increasing hostility to the AFL more than by a rational calculation of the new union's prospects. His own experience as a craft unionist, and then briefly in the industrially organized American Railway Union, had made him a lifelong foe of craft organization. He repeatedly pointed out how separate craft unions kept workers divided and weak. On the railroads, for example, Debs recounted how the telegraphers on the Missouri, Kansas & Texas Railway had gone out on strike, while the engineers, firemen, and trainmen kept working because their unions had unexpired contracts. The result was defeat and the firing of all 1,300 telegraphers on the MKT. Debs frequently cited this and other examples of how craft divisions weakened labor. He was convinced that the AFL was irretrievably committed to craft unionism.[4]

[4] See Schlesinger, *op. cit.*, pp. 171–241.

Equally important, Debs argued, was the association of AFL leaders with the leaders of large corporations and with bourgeois politicians in the National Civic Federation (NCF). The NCF had been organized in 1900 to promote conservative, responsible unionism and to win big businessmen to an appreciation of the inevitability of unionism and the desirability of union loyalty to corporate capitalism. As Debs said, the NCF was organized "for the one purpose of dovetailing the interests of labor and capital, and every member of this body insists that these interests can be harmonized." That was what Samuel Gompers, head of the AFL said, and that was what John Mitchell, president of the United Mine Workers, said. And this despite the fact that the "only purpose" of the NCF was "by subtle schemes to reduce the trade union movement to harmless impotency." This was the NCF's "real mission." By falling "within the fatal influence of this emasculating alliance," Debs insisted, the AFL has "proven that it is not organized to advance the true interests of the working class." [5]

If the "supreme purpose" of the NCF was to prolong "the agelong sleep of the working class," the IWW had been "organized for an opposite purpose": to tell the workers "that there can be no peace between you, the working class, and the capitalist class who exploit you." The working class had "economic interests apart from and opposed to" the capitalists' interests. If workers were "intelligent enough to understand their interests," Debs argued, they would sever their relations with the old unions, in which they were "divided and subdivided, and join the Industrial Workers, in which all are organized and united upon the basis of the class struggle." [6]

Debs was speaking only six months after the IWW founding convention and mostly from hope and determination rather than actual experience. Thus he could claim that the new union already had approximately 100,000 dues-paying members and that applications for charters and organizers were coming "from every direction." When the delegates of "this revolutionary economic organization meet in the city of Chicago, next year," Debs said, "it will be the greatest convention that ever met in the United States." [7]

[5] *Ibid.*, pp. 178–179.
[6] *Ibid.*, p. 226.
[7] *Ibid.*, p. 229.

But when the IWW's second convention did meet in 1906, only ninety-three delegates were present, the total membership was less than 60,000, and 27,000 of these were members of the WFM, which was about to pull out. And, of course, it was at this convention that the Socialists and WFM forces were defeated by De Leon and his ''anarchist'' allies. Debs had argued against participation in the AFL in 1905 and had even suggested that the United Mine Workers of America had ''run its course'' and was ''practically in charge of the mine owners.'' The only way the miners could ''get away from that situation,'' Debs said, was to ''sever their relations with that capitalist-controlled union and join and build up one of their own upon the basis of class struggle.'' Trying to change the UMW from the inside, bringing it ''to its proper position by 'boring from within,' '' was hopeless—''historically impossible.''

This flirtation with dual unionism did not last long. By 1910 Debs was declaring that ''we should bore from within and without,'' that industrial unionists in the old unions should work in harmony with those building new revolutionary industrial unions. However, there was nobody building revolutionary industrial unions. The IWW, despite its leadership of spontaneous militant strikes—the most famous and successful of which was at Lawrence, Massachusetts, in 1912—did not grow or establish a stable membership.[8] Instead, IWW activity increasingly centered on dual unionism in the mining industry. This combination of organizational weakness and attacks on the established unions brought Debs into open conflict with the IWW during a bitter coal strike in the Cabin Creek area of West Virginia.

The pro-IWW editor of the Huntington (West Virginia) *Socialist and Labor Star* attacked Debs for supporting the UMW officials. In an unusually sharp retort, Debs declared that although he was an industrial unionist, he was ''not an industrial bummerite.'' The ''real enemies of the working class,'' Debs added, were the supporters of the IWW who were ''magnifying every petty complaint against the United Mine Workers and arousing suspicion against everyone connected with it.'' Unlike the IWW, which had ''never done one particle of organizing'' in

---

[8] After the war started in Europe and labor was scarce in the West, the IWW did build a large membership among migratory agricultural workers and lumber workers in 1915 and 1916. This success was destroyed by government prosecution of IWW leaders after the United States entered the war in 1917.

the "dangerous districts" of the state, Debs now argued that the UMW had "been on the job for years," was a stable organization, and was "steadily evolving into a thoroughly industrial union." "Never in a thousand years," said Debs, would "these disrupters" of the IWW organize West Virginia coal miners—or, for that matter, those of "any other state." [9]

Debs' more friendly view toward the UMW was partly a result of the IWW's failure to meet his expectations, but Socialist activity within the miners union from 1905 to 1913 was also partly responsible. For while Debs was advocating opposition to the UMW from 1905 to 1908, other Socialists were boring from within and gaining strength in the union. This was reflected when the 1911 UMW convention passed a resolution making membership in the National Civic Federation a cause for expulsion from the union. As a result, John Mitchell, former UMW president, was forced to resign his position as chairman of the Trade Agreements Committee of the NCF, and (again in 1912) John H. Walker, a Socialist and president of the Illinois district of the UMW, was elected president of the Illinois Federation of Labor. By 1914, Debs had long given up on the IWW. But he still believed that to change the AFL as a whole was impossible, and so he remained an advocate of a new federation of "revolutionary" industrial unions. This time, his hopes were pinned on the UMW as the center of a new federation. When the WFM proposed a merger to the 1914 UMW convention, Debs enthusiastically endorsed the idea. Many years later, in 1935, the UMW would indeed become the center of a new federation of industrial unions (the CIO), but in 1914, partly because the WFM was in such poor shape, the UMW turned down the proposal. Thus, from 1914 on, Debs had no practical perspective for Socialist activity in relation to the unions.

Given the inability of the IWW to build its own organization, there were two alternative perspectives open to those who considered themselves revolutionaries. The syndicalist alternative was simply to work within the AFL in the belief that trade union experience in itself was radicalizing. The Socialist alternative was to build the party as the revo-

---

[9] See W. H. Thompson, "How a Victory Was Turned into a 'Settlement' in West Virginia," *International Socialist Review,* vol. XIV, no. 1 (July 1913), pp. 12 ff. and "Debs Denounces Critics," *ibid.,* vol. XIV, no. 2 (August 1913), p. 105.

lutionary organization, while remaining active within the existing center of trade unionism and conducting whatever struggles were possible there to move toward industrial unionism, and to develop socialist consciousness among the organized workers.

Syndicalism was advocated and practiced by William Z. Foster and others in the Syndicalist League, which Foster organized in 1912 after trying to convince the IWW to give up its dual unionism. Foster had joined the IWW a year after quitting the Socialist Party in 1909, but after a trip to Europe in 1911, where he observed the success of French and English radicals working within the established unions, he became convinced that the IWW should be dissolved as a dual union and reorganized as an educational league of activists within the various AFL affiliates.

Foster did not abandon the IWW because he had lost faith in revolutionary unionism, but because the IWW had failed to organize more than 10,000 to 15,000 workers (while the AFL and Railroad brotherhoods had about 2,500,000), and because he believed that revolutionary consciousness and organization could be created through militant trade unionism even of the AFL variety. He now "bitterly" opposed the "international Socialist Party," which he saw as "an interloper and a parasite" on the unions and believed the party should be fought as an enemy.[10]

In February 1912, Foster paid his last dues to the IWW and joined the AFL union of his craft, the Brotherhood of Railway Carmen, in Chicago. During the next few years, he worked to build the Syndicalist League and as a craft unionist in the Chicago Federation of Labor (CFL). He quickly gained prominence in his union and in the CFL, which was led by John Fitzpatrick. In 1917, with Fitzpatrick as chairman, Foster served as secretary to the Stockyards Labor Council in a successful effort to unionize the major packing companies, which had been strongly anti-union.

Several factors contributed to Foster's success in organizing the packinghouse workers in late 1917. Foster's and Fitzpatrick's militant and talented leadership were important, but so were the wartime labor shortages and the government's wartime policy of conciliation toward

[10] See William English Walling, "Industrialism vs. Syndicalism," *International Socialist Review*, vol. XIII, no. 9 (March 1913), pp. 666–667.

the AFL—in exchange for all-out support of the war effort by the unions. The final victory in the packing industry came when the unions threatened to strike for recognition in December 1917. To prevent an interruption of production, the President's Mediation Commission rushed to Chicago and secured a no-strike agreement that provided for a federal administrator to arbitrate the issues. Three months later, in late March 1918, the administrator handed down an award granting the packing-house workers the eight-hour day with ten hours' pay, overtime after eight hours, and other concessions.[11]

Success in the packing industry encouraged Foster to propose an organizing drive in the steel industry. His resolution at a meeting of the Chicago Federation of Labor was unanimously adopted and forwarded to AFL headquarters in Washington, and at the next AFL convention (June 1918) Foster moved that a conference be called during the convention to discuss such a drive. Three large meetings were held and a National Committee for Organizing Iron and Steel Workers was created, again with Fitzpatrick as the functioning chairman (Gompers was nominal chairman) and Foster as secretary-treasurer.

Interestingly, considering the commitment of IWW's, Socialists, and other radicals to industrial organization, the packinghouse workers were organized into the several existing craft unions. Similarly, when the steel organizing drive was proposed neither Foster nor anyone else suggested an industrial union. This conservative approach was later defended by Foster as "best fitted to get results at this stage in the development of the unions and the packing industry."[12] During the year after the organizing committee was established, Foster directed activities in and around the nation's steel mills, and in September 1919 the Great Steel Strike began. More than 250,000 steelworkers struck, about half the industry's work force. The walkout was only partial, but in some areas it was almost completely effective, and in any case it exceeded in magnitude and scope anything in American trade unionism's experience.

But by 1919 the war was over, and with it labor shortages and the need for full production and concessions to "responsible" trade union-

[11] David Brody, *Labor in Crisis* (Philadelphia and New York, 1965), p. 61.

[12] William Z. Foster, *The Great Steel Strike and Its Lessons* (New York, 1920), p. 20. Also cited in Brody, *ibid.*, p. 64.

ists. Gompers had presumably embraced the idea of a steel organizing drive in 1918 in anticipation that the organizing would be done under wartime conditions of cooperation between the government and the unions. But the war ended too soon, and Gompers himself began to lose interest in the steel campaign. This situation was made worse by public attacks on Foster for his radical syndicalism. When Foster appeared before a Senate committee investigating the strike, he was questioned extensively about his revolutionary beliefs, which he only partially repudiated. This testimony further divided Foster and Gompers and strengthened the hand of the companies in their campaign to smear the strike as a Bolshevik plot.

In the face of adamant opposition from United States Steel, and the unwillingness of the government to intervene in behalf of the strikers (as it had done during the packinghouse strike), the result was preordained. Strengthened by five years of wartime profits—abnormally high even for big steel—the companies could have withstood even a complete shutdown, which not even Foster had thought possible. Within a month or two it was clear to all concerned that the strike was lost, and although it dragged on until early 1920, it ended in total defeat.

Despite this experience, Foster insisted that the trade unions were "making straight for the abolition of capitalism . . . incomparably faster . . .. than any of the much-advertised, so-called revolutionary unions." He saw the IWW as "idealistic and utopian," and argued, from his own experience, that the "power of even a few" men "proceeding intelligently along practical lines is one of the marvels of the labor movement." [13] From the point of view of organizing workers into unions, Foster had the best of the argument with the IWW. It had failed both as a union and as a revolutionary organization. Indeed, in actual organizing situations, especially between 1915 and 1917 when it organized tens of thousands of migratory agricultural workers and lumber workers, the IWW had consistently played down its revolutionary purpose and limited itself to immediate union demands. But if Foster had been able to organize workers into stable unions, where the IWW could not, what about his private purpose: the building of a revolutionary movement? In this, despite his intentions, Foster had even less to show than did the IWW.

[13] Foster, *ibid.*, p. 262; also cited by Brody, *ibid.*, pp. 142–143.

The failure to build revolutionary unions, either inside or outside the AFL, was not the result of a failure of will either on the part of the IWW or of Foster and people like him within the AFL. To succeed in organizing the masses of workers, a union had to address the grievances and state of mind of the majority of workers in a given industry. In a situation where only a small percentage of the workers were Socialists, a "revolutionary union"—one that insisted on placing its anti-capitalist politics at the center of its activity—could not expect to organize large numbers of workers. The exceptions to this generalization were always transitory and were the result of special circumstances. A good example was the Pressed Steel Car Company strike at McKees Rocks, Pennsylvania, in 1909. The workers at McKees Rocks spontaneously went out on strike to protest a wage cut. In desperate need for experienced and skilled organizers, their requests for help went unanswered by the AFL. Although the IWW had no local at McKees Rocks, it nevertheless went in to help organize three weeks after the strike began. The IWW was welcomed by the strikers because it was able to provide day-to-day help in the form of organizers who could speak in the ten different languages of the immigrant workers. The skill of the IWW in unifying the workers and providing tactical leadership won the union thousands of members. But once the strike was over, on terms partly favorable to the workers, the IWW dissolved in the area.

Similarly, at Lawrence, Massachusetts, in 1912, the IWW became involved in a strike of more than 20,000 textile workers, mostly women, of many different nationalities. The strike began spontaneously over a wage cut. This time there was a small Italian-speaking IWW local on the scene and IWW organizers arrived almost immediately. Lawrence was the IWW's greatest victory, won in part through cooperation with the Socialists, who helped give the strike publicity both by sending children of the strikers to homes of sympathetic Socialists in New York, Philadelphia, and other cities, and through hearings in the House of Representatives called by Victor Berger, then a Socialist congressman from Milwaukee. But as at McKees Rocks, the Lawrence local grew phenomenally during the strike and then quickly dwindled to a handful once the strike was over and things were back to normal.

By defining themselves as outside of and opposed to capitalist society, the IWW could not become a stable union—at least not under the conditions that existed in the early 1900s. But, conversely, by working within the AFL simply as militant trade unionists, the syndicalists could not move the workers toward socialism or "revolution." Precisely because a union's function is to defend the interests of workers as workers it must operate within capitalist social relations. It must accept the wage system, work within it, and get the best possible deal for the workers at any given moment. Thus the union itself cannot be the basis of revolutionary consciousness. To the degree that it functions as a union—that is, settles for wage increases, improves conditions, signs contracts and assumes responsibility for their enforcement—the union cannot by itself be revolutionary. And, as the IWW discovered, to the degree that a union does not function this way, it does not become a stable or powerful organization—it is not recognized and is bitterly opposed by corporations and the state.

Ironically, Foster's syndicalism—his rejection of the need for a party that stands for socialism in society at large—dovetailed perfectly with classical revisionism in the socialist movement. In Germany, which had the largest Socialist Party in the world until after World War I, the leadership of the trade unions and of the Socialist Party (which had organized the unions) increasingly merged. The trade unionists gradually came to dominate the party; their goals became the goals of the party as a whole. Edward Bernstein, who believed that socialism would evolve out of an inevitable process of reform, argued that for Socialists the ultimate aim was nothing, but that the actual movement—the party and the unions—was everything. Trade unionism and parliamentary reform, the improvement of the workers' daily lot, would simply develop until the character of society changed from capitalist to socialist. But to the extent that Socialists did not constantly bring the ultimate aim of socialism into the unions and did not organize outside the unions to transform society as a whole, socialism and socialist consciousness in the unions were increasingly subordinated to their function as bargaining agent for workers within the framework of capitalism. In the absence of a revolutionary "ultimate aim," brought to the workers from outside their day-to-day experience, the unions inevitably came to accept the ultimate aim of the capitalists: the perpetuation of corporate capitalism and the continued subordination of the working class.

In short, if the unions were to be won to the revolution it would be necessary for a socialist party to exist on the outside and to represent and lead the struggle for a new society. The majority in the Socialist Party in the United States understood this necessity. They generally opposed the IWW as a dual union and saw their function in relation to the unions not primarily as organizers—though Socialists were instrumental in organizing many unions—but as supporters of the existing unions. The basis of Socialist strength within the unions was the party's public presence outside the unions, its visible intention to take power in society at large. To the degree that the party opposed the capitalists where they functioned together as a class—that is, in government bodies on municipal, state, and federal levels—Socialists were also able to function openly and effectively as Socialists in the unions. Until the war, those Socialists who worked within the AFL did so with considerable success. Socialist trade unionists were often elected to public office in these years. Thomas Van Lear, a machinist, was elected mayor of Minneapolis in 1916, for example. And James H. Maurer was elected to the State Assembly in Pennsylvania in 1910 and then became president of that state's federation of labor in 1912. Similarly, John H. Walker, a Socialist miner, became president of the Illinois Federation of Labor in 1912 and was his party's candidate for mayor of Danville in 1915.

The War and the Russian Revolution

World War I and the Russian Revolution changed the character of the socialist movement in the United States as in the rest of the world. The almost universal support given to wartime governments by European socialist parties in 1914 shocked and disillusioned millions of party members and sympathizers and made it clear that there was something profoundly wrong with the movement. The result was the collapse of the Second International, a widespread realization of the reformist character of European social democracy, and the emergence of the Communist movement and the Third International as the dominant force on the left in the following decades.

The United States did not enter the war until 1917, three years after it had started, and then the American Socialist Party consistently opposed American participation. A few party members, mostly journalists, writers, and trade union leaders, supported the war effort and took the lead in denouncing their former comrades as German agents. These people either resigned or were expelled from the party for their pro-war activity. The great majority of Socialists campaigned actively against the war, against conscription, and for an open declaration of war aims and an immediate peace. Their activity struck a responsive chord among millions of Americans who opposed the war. Congress declared a state of war in April, and immediately thereafter and through the November elections, the party held mass meetings of unprecedented size and campaigned in city after city against the war. The result was amazing.

In Wisconsin, for example, a local Republican newspaper reported that "probably no party ever gained more rapidly in strength than the Socialist Party is just at the present time." In places where "ordinarily a few hundred are considered large assemblages," the paper continued, "thousands assemble to hear Socialist speakers." Indeed, it now appeared that the Socialists could "carry Sheboygan County by three to one against the two old parties together." [14] Of course, Wisconsin was largely inhabited by German immigrants, so anti-war sentiment there was to be expected. But the Wisconsin experience was not unique. In Dayton, Ohio, the Socialists conducted an anti-war campaign in the primary election in August and won an absolute majority in a three-way contest, winning the largest plurality in the city's history. This and similar results in various other cities prompted the Akron (Ohio) *Beacon-Journal*, a conservative Republican newspaper, to comment that there was "scarcely a political observer whose opinion is worth much but what will admit that were an election to come now a mighty tide of Socialism would innundate the Middle West"—and "maybe all other sections of this country." [15]

But precisely because the party's anti-war activity gained such widespread support and showed the potential for rapid growth of a Socialist-led anti-war movement, it brought down upon the party the wrath of the Wilson Administration, as well as attacks from organized business groups. These took several forms, but the most damaging were the indictment and conviction of some 2,000 Socialists under the wartime espionage and sedition acts and the banning and removal from the mails of dozens of Socialist and other radical newspapers and magazines. As a result of this repression, the party apparatus was greatly weakened and a shift in its active membership occurred. Some 1,500

[14] *Plymouth* (Wisconsin) *Review,* August 29, 1917.
[15] Akron *Beacon-Journal,* September 7, 1917.

party locals, almost all of them in the rural and small town areas of the South and Midwest, where Socialists were relatively isolated and vulnerable, were destroyed. This happened at the same time that locals in the larger industrial cities, especially those located in the North, from Boston to Minneapolis, were able to recruit thousands of new members. In many of the non-industrial states, the party organizations were destroyed by concerted attacks on Socialists on the farm or in small towns. And in Oklahoma, where an uprising of some 1,200 farmers took place in August 1917 (known as the Green Corn Rebellion), the state party formally dissolved itself after Victor Berger and four other national leaders were indicted under the Espionage Act in 1918.[16] This was done out of fear that the prosecution might draw a connection between the Green Corn Rebellion and the activities of the party leadership.

Although the party had anticipated some of the attacks that opposing the war would bring down upon itself, it was able to take a strong anti-war stand initially and to continue its anti-war stand for several reasons. First, the United States did not enter the war until three years after it began, and so the American party had time to debate the war and its character and to assess the positions taken by the European Socialists. The debates within the party produced a widely shared understanding of the war as an imperialist contest over markets and colonies. This conclusion was facilitated by the fact that the American party, unlike the major European parties, had a diverse membership with substantial numbers of immigrants (or children of immigrants) from countries on both sides of the conflict.

In addition, because the party was relatively independent of the trade unions (whereas the European parties had become largely the political expression of their trade union movements), it was able to chart its own course. Many American trade union Socialists, almost all in leadership positions in the various unions, did support the war. William H. Johnston, for example, a Socialist and president of the Machinists union, supported the war and quit the party. Other unions, most notably the Amalgamated Clothing Workers, formally opposed the war in order to appease its Socialist membership but in fact cooperated fully with the Wilson Administration. In fact, it was impossible for a union to oppose

[16] Berger was indicted in the middle of his 1918 campaign for the U.S. Senate. He received 26 percent of the vote in the election.

the war and survive. Production had to be maintained without interruption. This was a life-and-death matter for the ruling class. Serious union opposition to the war—a refusal to produce—would have been an insurrectionary act, one that would have been possible only if the unions had been solidly Socialist and the party had been strong enough to move toward taking power. Neither was the case, of course, so the unions had to cooperate or be destroyed.

The IWW tried to avoid this choice by ignoring the war. It did not oppose the war and in fact saw it as a diversionary issue. Before the United States entered the war, an IWW leader wrote that his war aim would be for the "One Big Union" to "come out of the conflict stronger and with more industrial control than previously." Why, he asked, should the IWW "sacrifice working class interests for the sake of a few noisy and impotent parades or anti-war demonstrations?" He preferred to "get on the job of organizing the working class to take over the industries, war or no war, and stop all future capitalist aggression that leads to war and other forms of barbarism." [17] In letters to other IWW leaders, Haywood, too, argued against becoming involved in anti-war activity, especially since to do so would open the union to government attack. "The world war," he wrote, "is of small importance compared to the great class war." And to a group of Wobblies in Detroit, Haywood admonished: "Keep cool and confine your agitation to job control." This was the real issue and there was "no need of going on record for or against any movement that arises from other sources." [18]

Official neutrality on the war, however, did not save the IWW from wartime repression. Indeed, a few days before the actual declaration of war state militiamen and "off-duty" United States Marines raided IWW headquarters in Kansas City and destroyed the union's papers and office furnishings. Kansas City police watched the proceedings and then left in the company of the soldiers. [19] This attack was a small harbinger of things to come. Once the United States was in the war, the IWW became a prime target of vigilantes. One IWW orga-

[17] Quoted in Melvin Dubofsky, *We Shall Be All* (Chicago, 1969), p. 353.
[18] See Joseph R. Conlin, *Big Bill Haywood and the Radical Union Movement* (Syracuse, 1969), p. 183.
[19] Dubofsky, *op. cit.,* p. 383.

nizer, Frank Little, was dragged from his hotel room in Butte, Montana, in August 1917, and was mutilated and hung from a railroad trestle. In Bisbee, Arizona, some 1,200 striking IWW copper miners and sympathizers were stuffed into boxcars and taken several hundred miles into the desert, where they were dumped and prevented from returning to their homes and families. Finally, the federal government indicted, tried, and convicted almost the entire IWW leadership in two trials, one in Chicago and the other in Sacramento, involving more than 250 union men.

While the IWW was thus being destroyed, the government moved to meet the grievances of workers who were being organized by the radical union. The most striking example was in the lumber industry of the Northwest, where as the IWW was smashed, the government set up its own union, the Loyal Legion of Loggers and Lumbermen, and imposed drastically improved conditions (including the eight-hour day) on the industry. This government-company union produced a more docile labor force and assured uninterrupted production of Sitka spruce, an essential raw material for the then-infant airplane industry.

The treatment of the AFL contrasted sharply with that of the IWW. Eagerly and fully cooperating with the war effort, the AFL was given unprecedented recognition by Wilson. For the first time in American history, representatives of organized labor were given seats on government bodies during the war. Hugh Frayne of the AFL sat as a member of the War Industries Board, and Gompers himself headed the Labor Committee of the Council of National Defense. In this situation, such syndicalists as William Z. Foster could not afford even the neutrality of the IWW on the war. Working within the AFL, and directly under Gompers as an organizer in the packing industry, Foster made "dozens" of speeches urging workers to support the war by buying Liberty Bonds.[20]

The party was the only major political organization to oppose the war, and in the minds of millions of people its analysis made good sense even during the war. For years after 1919, despite its breakup and decline, the party's wartime stand and activities remained its great-

[20] Testimony of William Z. Foster at *Investigation of Strike in Steel Industry*, Hearings before the Committee on Education and Labor, U.S. Senate, 66th Congress, First Session (Washington, D.C., 1919), p. 423.

est political assets. But three things prevented the resurgence of the Socialist Party and of a large-scale popular movement for socialism after World War I. The first was the government attacks on the party and its press during the war. The second was a generally shaken faith in the traditional theory of the party and in the international movement. The party's optimism about a trade unionist political perspective was undermined by the ease with which the trade unions had abandoned any long-range or class-conscious perspective. Similarly, the ease with which the government used reforms to weaken support for the radicals—as, for example, when it smashed the IWW and imposed an eight-hour day on the lumber industry—brought into question the relationship of immediate demands to ultimate ends.

Even Victor Berger, right-wing Socialist from Wisconsin and formerly one of the strongest advocates of working within the AFL in order to convert its members to socialism, believed the war had strengthened *"treason* within the working class." Both publicly and privately, Berger reversed himself with regard to the AFL and the IWW (which he had militantly opposed before the war). To an IWW leader, Berger wrote in 1918 that he was "beginning to believe that the IWW (or some labor organization that will succeed it but that will inherit its matchless spirit) is destined to take the place of the AFL in our country and fulfill the mission in which the AFL has failed." And Berger's paper, the Milwaukee *Leader,* editorialized a short time later that the IWW might "have a brilliant future as a labor organization." "Certainly," it added, "there is abundant room for a real labor organization in the industrial field in this country—one that is loyal to the working class—one that will not barter its principles for a few dollars and fishes—one that understands the ultimate as well as the immediate needs of the workers." [21]

The war and the Russian Revolution also undermined the confidence that Socialists had in winning power through the electoral process. Berger still believed that socialism would come in the United States "by means of the ballot." But he believed that millions of people had learned "that it was capitalism that caused the war, and that capital-

---

[21] Berger to Morris Hillquit, Milwaukee, August 20, 1919, Hillquit papers, Wisconsin State Historical Society; James Weinstein, *The Decline of Socialism in America, 1912–1925* (New York, 1967), p. 178; Milwaukee *Leader,* September 3, 1918.

ism is likely to keep on causing wars until it is replaced by socialism." To Berger, this meant that "either before the war is over or soon after, the common people" would "take possession of the various governments *either by means of the ballot or otherwise,* and establish social democracy." If Berger still had a parliamentary perspective, though with far less certainty than before the war, a left-wing Socialist like Charles E. Ruthenberg saw a positive need to break "with American methods and American ideals." When Socialists presented the party's view of the war at public meetings and in electoral campaigns, Ruthenberg pointed out, "they went to prison by the thousands." And in Cleveland, when three Socialists elected to city office in 1917 refused to pledge support to the war, they were expelled from the council. "If the Socialists are seeking new weapons," Ruthenberg concluded, "it is because the ruling class has taught them the need of new weapons." [22]

Third, in this situation the effect of the Russian Revolution was sharply to polarize the Socialist movement, not only in Europe (where most Socialist parties joined their bourgeois governments during the war), but also in the United States. Among American Socialists, support for the Revolution and opposition to Allied intervention against the Bolsheviks was strong. Virtually all party members enthusiastically and joyfully supported the Soviets. But the implications of the Revolution—as explained by the newly formed Communist International in 1919—for socialist politics in the United States caused deep divisions. By 1919 the old party had split into three parties—the Socialist, Communist, and Communist Labor—and some smaller groupings.

[22] *Ohio Socialist,* April 9, 1919, quoted in Weinstein, *ibid.,* p. 200.

2/

BREAKUP OF THE MOVEMENT AND
THE EMERGENCE OF THE COMMUNIST PARTY

Russia and the United States

The splitting of the Socialist Party followed from differences about the possibility of immediate insurrection in the United States. Those who were to remain Socialists pointed out that conditions in the United States were entirely different from those that made insurrection possible in Russia in 1917. As Berger argued, Russia had been a "beaten country" both militarily and economically. Her army was all but destroyed and was "honeycombed with propaganda." Russian Socialists controlled the trade unions, and the peasants, Berger added, were ready to revolt against their feudal masters but had no party to turn to except the Bolsheviks. In contrast, various Socialist leaders insisted, capitalism in the United States had been strengthened by the war. The trade union movement had been purged of Socialists, and the party had been weakened. Although there was considerable postwar disillusionment with the "war for democracy," there was no indication that any substantial numbers of workers or farmers were ready to revolt.[1]

Those who became Communists never confronted these argu-

[1] James Weinstein, *The Decline of Socialism in America, 1912–1925* (New York, 1967), Ch. 4.

ments. They simply accepted the call of the New International to take up insurrectionary politics. For the Bolsheviks this demand had a compelling logic. Socialist revolution had always been thought to be possible only in the more highly industrialized nations—those that had the industrial and cultural base for an economy of abundance. When Lenin argued for a seizure of power by the Bolsheviks, it was "in order to kindle a Socialist Revolution in Europe." Both aspects of this idea shocked his comrades. But if the Bolshevik Revolution did not set off a revolutionary wave in Western Europe, Lenin believed, the prospects for maintaining the Revolution in Russia were poor. Indeed, as late as 1922 Lenin proclaimed "this elementary truth of Marxism, that the victory of socialism *requires* the joint efforts of workers in a number of *advanced* countries." [2] Thus, when the Bolsheviks seized power in Russia they believed that the Revolution must spread, and that when it did the leadership of the revolutionary movement would revert to the West (where it belonged) because the proletariat there was more highly developed. For two or three years after 1917, the Bolsheviks believed that they were doomed if the Revolution did not spread to the West. From this point of view, the International's insistence that affiliation required an insurrectionary program was not arbitrary. A party that professed support of the Revolution but did not move toward the seizure of power appeared "objectively" anti-Soviet: it was unwilling to do what was necessary to the survival of the Revolution in Russia.

The unwillingness of the established leadership in the American Socialist Party to accept an insurrectionary outlook was the immediate cause of the split in 1919. At that time, two new parties, the Communist and Communist Labor parties, formed and immediately joined the Third International. At its Emergency Convention in September 1919, the majority of the Socialist Party opposed affiliation; later however, after a membership referendum upheld the "minority" position in favor of joining, the party applied for membership. In rejecting the Socialist Party's application, Gregory Zinoviev, president of the International, insisted that it was "not a hotel," where anyone could go with his own

[2] Quoted in Theodore Draper, *The Roots of American Communism* (New York, 1957), p. 98, and Moshe Lewin, *Lenin's Last Struggle* (New York, 1969), p. 4. Emphasis in the original.

baggage, but "an army in wartime." Those who joined this "Army of Revolution," Zinoviev explained, "must adopt as their program the program of the Communist International—open and revolutionary mass struggle for Communism through the Dictatorship of the Proletariat by means of the workers' Soviets." Furthermore, they must "create a strongly centralized form of organization, a military discipline," and all party members "must be absolutely subject to the full-powered Central Committee of the Party." In addition, they must "prepare for revolutionary action, for merciless civil war." [3]

The debate over immediate insurrection and over affiliation with the Communist International did not advance the socialist movement in the United States. Rather, it diverted Socialists from considering their wartime experiences and the increasing stagnation of the party in the face of a developing liberal corporatism. There was some new thinking before the split by those who later became Communists, although it was vague and limited. This advance, stimulated by the Bolshevik seizure of power, was around the concept of mass action, which, according to Louis Fraina, a leading left-wing Socialist Party theoretician, meant bringing "mass proletarian pressure on the capitalist state" by shifting the center of activity from the parliaments to the shops and the streets, making electoral activity only one phase of Socialist politics. [4]

But Communist leaders, including Fraina, retained the Socialist Party's historical determinism. While Fraina understood the necessity of developing new concepts of direct rule, and shared Lenin's vision of the Soviets as a transitional form of the state, he had little else to offer. He believed that the crisis of American capitalism would proceed apace, and that revolutionaries needed simply to wait and prepare themselves for the seizure of power. In less thoughtful hands the limitations of this perspective were more apparent. William F. Dunne, editor of the Butte *Daily Bulletin* and a founder of the Communist Labor Party, argued in 1919 that "craft unionism is out of date; it is too late for industrial unionism; mass action is the only thing—mass action." Dunne then predicted that "unemployment will increase, there'll be starvation, and

---

[3] See Weinstein, *op. cit.*, Ch. 4.

[4] *The New York Communist,* vol. 1, no. 2 (April 1919); quoted in James Weinstein, "The Underdevelopment of Socialism in Advanced Industrial Society," *Socialist Revolution,* January–February 1970.

someday the banks will fail and the people will come pouring out on the streets and the revolution will start.'' [5]

These views came in part from the social turmoil in the United States in 1919—the Seattle General Strike had already occurred, the Boston Police Strike and the Great Steel Strike were only months away. But more important was the euphoria created by the Russian Revolution and the way the Bolsheviks had defied social-democratic theory in willfully seizing power. In traditional Marxist theory, revolution would occur first in an advanced capitalist country, one in which the working class was the major class and in which the workers had become committed to socialism through parliamentary and trade union activity. Yet the Bolsheviks had seized power in a pre-industrial nation where the working class was relatively small and an open Socialist movement was illegal. Dunne's scenario reflected his understanding of what had happened in Russia—and what he hoped would happen in the United States. But he, and the others like him who became Communists in 1919, overlooked the central fact in Lenin's departure from the orthodox Marxist tradition: that Russia, unlike the United States, was still a semi-feudal nation at the time of the Revolution. Socialist consciousness was meaningless in Russia except to the tiny percentage of the population who were workers. For the overwhelming peasant majority, the enemies were landed proprietors and the czarist bureaucrats. The peasants supported the Bolsheviks to get land for themselves, not to establish socialism. But in the United States, where the majority of the population was already in the working class, unity in support of the revolution could be achieved only on the basis of opposition to corporate capitalism and for a socialist society. Dunne assumed what was at issue: the need for mass socialist consciousness among the workers. His scenario could work only if the majority of working people already understood the need for socialism before "the banks failed." Then, if they came pouring out into the streets it would be to seize power in their own right. Otherwise, as it happened in 1929 and after, if they came pouring out into the streets it would only be to reopen the banks.

Lenin had argued just after the turn of the century that the czarist autocracy in Russia had blocked the "development of capitalism as a

---

[5] Quoted in Weinstein, *Decline*, p. 206.

whole'' and had thus created a revolutionary "liberal opposition," a movement of capitalists and their allies against the semi-feudalism of the Czar.[6] Seeing this development as positive, some Socialists believed their primary responsibility was to subordinate Socialist agitation in favor of support for the liberal revolution, as a progressive step in Russian evolution. Others saw the liberal movement against the existing autocracy as simply "bourgeois" and therefore as of no interest to the working class. Lenin's unique contribution lay in seeing that the demands for liberalization by bourgeois and peasant forces were positive and useful for the working-class movement. He believed the Socialists should work with the liberal revolutionaries and try to convert the bourgeois revolution into a Socialist revolution. This could be done if the Socialists constantly took the initiative. Believing in the "proletarian revolutionary character of the age," Lenin argued that in Russia (and, as it turned out, also in the semi-colonies of Asia) the demands of the bourgeois revolution could only be "realized within the framework of proletarian revolution." In short, Lenin believed that proletarian revolution in Russia meant "at one and the same time the realization and the suppression of the bourgeois revolution." This was possible because the Czar had failed to win the support of the masses, and the capitalists were too scattered and weak to do so. In this respect, the situation in Russia was much more like that in the colonies and semi-colonies than in Europe or in the United States where the bourgeoisie had firmly established its control and consolidated its rule.[7]

Lenin's concept of the party in 1902 and its role followed from this analysis. Since Russia was a pre-bourgeois, or semi-bourgeois, society, the industrial working class, on which the party was based, constituted only a thin layer of society. The overwhelming majority of the oppressed were peasants, handicraftsmen, or petty artisans, not industrial workers. And the consciousness of these groups, if revolutionary, was bourgeois: they wanted land of their own and a liberal state apparatus. They had "general [i.e., bourgeois] democratic needs."[8] The idea of socialism was "natural" only to the working class, since it was the only class that had already experienced bourgeois social relations and could

[6] V. I. Lenin, "The Class Point of View," *Collected Works,* Vol. 4 (New York, 1929), pp. 84–85.

[7] *Ibid.,* pp. 28, 48, 49.

[8] V. I. Lenin, *What Is to Be Done?* (New York, 1961), p. 87.

easily understand the need to transcend them. But most workers in Russia were also illiterate. Science, including "social science" (Marxism), was the property of the middle class (the educated members of the petty bourgeoisie). And this meant that the idea of socialism, scientific Marxism, was initially available only to intellectuals from the middle class (like Lenin) and to the relatively few educated workers. Revolutionary intellectuals were not part of the working class but were professional revolutionaries who, along with a part of the working class, formed the party. From this situation the concept of a "vanguard" party arose. "Be it remembered," Lenin wrote, "that in order to *become* the vanguard, we [the party] must attract other classes." [9] The task of Socialists in Russia was twofold. First, while the party was still very small it devoted itself "exclusively to activities among the workers" and condemned "any deviation" that might prevent the creation of a socialist consciousness *within* the working class. Second, and only after a socialist consciousness had been diffused through the working class, it became the party's responsibility to "guide" the activities of various bourgeois or peasant opposition strata toward the "overthrow of the autocracy," with the aim of gaining state power by the vanguard class. [10]

The particular form of the party was further determined by the absence of bourgeois democracy, by the fact that working-class organizations—unions and parties—were illegal. Since public agitation for socialism (or even for democratic rights) was suppressed by the police, the party had to be secret, highly mobile, and disciplined. Lenin insisted that to be a revolutionary in Russia, a Socialist must be adept in "his own professional art—the art of combatting the political police." [11]

The role of a vanguard in creating a socialist consciousness among the working class, as well as leading other classes, conflicted with the need to remain underground and secret. Maintaining contact with the masses and helping to shape the direction of popular (bourgeois) revolutionary activity required participation within many "organizations intended for wide membership," organizations that had to be "as loose and public as possible." But because socialist agitation was illegal, the

---

[9] *Ibid.,* p. 88. Emphasis added.
[10] *Ibid.,* pp. 84, 86.
[11] *Ibid.,* pp. 189, 200.

need for socialism could not always be put forward in these ''public'' organizations without endangering them and the Socialists within them. This presented a dilemma that Lenin solved by arguing that even though the wider organizations had limited aims, these aims would lead them into conflict with the czarist state and make clear the need for its overthrow. This was so even though the aims were not in themselves Socialist.

In 1917 the United States was as unlike Russia as any nation in the world. It had the most advanced bourgeois democracy, the strongest democratic ideology of the industrialized capitalist nations, and also a highly literate and technically advanced working class. Almost entirely lacking a feudal heritage, the United States had from its inception been an unambiguously bourgeois nation. In Russia, Lenin argued in 1907, the Revolution was ''bourgeois in content,'' while in the United States and Britain, ''bourgeois-democratic historical tasks were almost nonexistent.'' [12] To achieve socialism in Russia there would have to be two revolutions, the first against the Czar, the second against a weak and ineffective capitalist class.[13] But in the United States, where the ''vanguard class'' was already highly developed, and where workers enjoyed formal democratic rights (public education, the right to vote and to organize into unions), the problem was building a movement for socialism among the workers.

Lenin's view of the United States was not entirely accurate in that he did not take into account the condition of blacks or women (neither of which had the right to vote or other legal rights). But the United States was nevertheless strikingly different from Russia. By World War I, corporate capital was already expanding beyond industrial production into agriculture and distribution and was integrating almost all sectors of the population into its marketplace and work force. The war, and wartime labor shortages, brought the only major stratum of the population that remained in semi-feudal isolation—southern blacks—to northern cities in large numbers. In short, the process of proletarianization was well advanced and was accelerating. There were still groups that had

[12] V. I. Lenin, *Lenin Against Revisionism* (Moscow, 1972), pp. 61, 80.

[13] This is, in fact, what happened in 1917. The first revolution in March brought Kerensky to power. Unable to stabilize Russian society or to govern effectively, he was overthrown by the Bolsheviks in November.

not won their formal rights, but these were not moving toward revolution. The major political movement among women was for suffrage, for integration, and by the end of the war the victory of suffrage was assured. And among blacks the major movements were the NAACP, which stood for legal and political equality, and the Universal Negro Improvement Association (UNIA), led by Marcus Garvey, which stood for race pride and freedom for the African and West Indian colonies. The Garvey movement's main thrust was black separatism. And the UNIA's main project was to establish a base of black power through black-owned businesses. Neither the black movement nor the women's movement threatened the hegemony of the corporate liberal ruling class because both movements sought equality within capitalism—sought to achieve for themselves the already existing rights of the rest of the population.

In Russia, the Bolsheviks broke with the historical determinism of the Second International by seizing power in the midst of chaos, even though the process of capitalist industrialization had only just begun. They were able to do so because neither the Czar nor the nascent capitalist class had gained the ideological allegiance of the population. But the option of a small minority party seizing power was not open to Americans and would not be even in the midst of profound crisis, as the collapse of 1929 would demonstrate. Capitalist rule and capitalist modes of thought were too well entrenched and too widely diffused in the United States. And yet, in 1919 the American Communists, swept along by the momentum of the Russian Revolution and disillusioned with the old Socialist electoral perspective, mimicked the Bolsheviks even to the extent of going underground. The Palmer Raids of January 1920, as a result of which many Eastern European immigrant radicals were deported, reinforced the underground mentality. But the raids themselves were short-lived and unpopular, and their end did not produce any change in Communist policy.

The denunciation of all leftist groups that refused to follow their policies of secret organization, and the renunciation of all agitation around immediate demands resulted in the loss of 90 percent of the membership that the Communists had taken with them when the Socialist Party split in 1919. By 1921, under steady pressure from the Third International, the Communists emerged from underground and became a "legal party." Facing reentry into the real political world, even the party leadership had to admit that the Communists did "not exist as a factor in the class struggle." [14]

The shallowness of the Communists' critique of the Socialist Party then became apparent. Communists had willingly suffered extreme sectarian isolation for two years because they believed that they would soon emerge, as Lenin had, to assume the leadership of the masses ready to revolt. But they had no awareness of the prior need to develop a popular consciousness of the desirability and possibility of an alternative social order (socialism). Their only alternative to Socialist attempts at building a popular movement for socialism was the romanticism of underground life. And, therefore, when the Communists came up from underground to form the Workers Party in December 1921, the program of immediate demands that they adopted was simply a rehash of the Socialist demands of 1918 and 1920, minus any attempt to explain the need for socialism, except in terms lifted directly from the Bolsheviks. [15]

The last half of the 1920s was a period of continuing stagnation for the Socialist Party and of great internal turmoil for the Communists. As organizers of a popular movement for socialism, both parties reached a dead end in 1924. The Socialist Party had lost its young people and its identification with the world revolutionary movement to the Communists and was becoming increasingly anti-Soviet. It had squandered its few remaining resources in supporting Robert La Follette's candidacy for President as an independent in 1924, and its strength in the AFL continued to decline. The Communists were not much better off. Their major political asset was their identification with the Soviet Union, but that relationship also involved them in the intense factional struggles within the Soviet party, first between Stalin and Trotsky and then between Stalin and Zinoviev and Bukharin. The various factions within the Communist Party were so busy during these years trying to keep up with what was going on in Russia—and trying to line up with the winners—that they could pay little attention to developments in the United States. In most cases party policy simply followed the policy of the International—in fact it often was decided by the International and im-

[14] A. Rafael (Alexander Bittleman), "The Task of the Hour," *The Communist,* October 1920.

[15] See Weinstein, *Decline,* Ch. 4.

posed upon the American party. These years, which immediately followed Lenin's death in 1924, were the period of "Bolshevization" of the International and its constituent parties. The result was firmly to establish the distinctive forms of organization and modes of work that characterized the Communist Party for the coming decades. The form of party organization and the ultimate fate of Communist leaders, in other words, depended upon the struggles within the International and not on conditions within the United States or on the historical experience of the socialist movement.

The result of the Communist Party's relationship to the International was its adoption of the form of the "vanguard party." The form of a revolutionary party should follow from its historical function. The function of a revolutionary party in the United States is to unite an increasingly diversified and stratified working class—one that is a large majority of the population—around the need for socialism. Its purpose must be to develop a socialist consciousness among all sectors of the working class so that they can come together to oppose and overthrow capitalism. The form of the party should follow from the nature of the working class and its relation to other classes, but for the Communists the form of the party was simply a copy of the Bolshevik party. This form, which has come to be known as "Leninist," was not what Lenin or the Boleheviks preferred, but was forced upon them by the harsh realities of Russian underdevelopment. By insisting on the universal validity of the strategy and organizational forms that were historically specific to the Russian Revolution, the American party guaranteed that socialist consciousness would remain the property of a small, and isolated, elite.

As we have seen, Lenin's concept of a vanguard party followed from the need to gain power in a semi-feudal society in which the working class was a tiny minority. With the Bolshevik seizure of power in 1917, Lenin anticipated that the form of the party would change and that the division of labor between the party and the masses would gradually dissolve. At the height of popular participation in the Revolution, the Soviets (popular councils of workers and other classes) seemed destined to replace the party. In *State and Revolution,* published in 1917, Lenin talked of the Soviets as a transitional state, one that would smash the "machinery of oppression" of czarist rule—the army, the police, the bureaucracy—and permit "direct participation in the *democratic* organization of life of the state from the bottom up." [16] Yet, when the Revolution failed to spread to the West and the Civil War began, the Soviets all but ceased to function. The party was again isolated from the impoverished masses. As Lenin wrote, "The Soviets, which according to their program were organs of government *by the workers,* are in fact only organs of government *for the workers* by the most advanced section of the proletariat." [17] By the end of the Civil War (1921) the situation was even worse. The working class itself had been largely eliminated as casualties of the war or by dispersal back into the countryside after their factories were destroyed. Instead of a full democratic participation of workers and peasants in government, the party alone retained a socialist consciousness and exercised power. And instead of becoming less hierarchical and less centralized, the party moved in the opposite direction in order to defend its very existence. Bolsheviks and educated workers were so few that there were not enough to fill even the major portion of industrial management and government posts. Large numbers of former czarist officials had to be recruited to help govern. Revolutionaries became a small minority at what Lenin called "the summit of the power structure." [18] At the base and middle levels, hundreds of thousands of former czarist bureaucrats, although loyal to the new regime, continued to work in their habitual manner.

In this situation, the monolithic party, characterized by a prohibition of factions and discussion of fundamental problems, came into being. As Moshe Lewin points out, "The constantly alarming nature of the situation and the extension of the state of emergency required a constant mobilization of the cadres, their transfer from one front to another, or from a military task to an economic one and vice versa. No democratic procedure would have made these solutions possible. These methods, which were sanctioned in no way either by theory or statute," thus became the reality of party life. [19] These developments provided the basis for what later became known as Stalinism, and with Stalin's accession to power in 1924 this meaning of Bolshevism was gradually but inexorably imposed on the parties of the Third International.

[16] Quoted in Lewin, *op. cit.,* p. 4.
[17] *Ibid.,* quoted on p. 6.
[18] *Ibid.,* p. 9.
[19] *Ibid.,* p. 13.

Bolshevization of the Communist Party

Until mid-1924 the American Communist Party had an eclectic form of organization, in part a hangover from the old Socialist Party's structure and in part a copy of the Russian Communist Party. This formal eclecticism reflected a confusion in underlying political perspectives. The Socialist Party's structure prior to 1919 had followed from its belief that the working class would become a majority and that the Revolution consisted of developing a mass socialist consciousness through parliamentary activity. Parliamentary activity for the old Socialist Party was both a means of educating the workers about the need for socialism and a path to power. Its revolutionary content was located in its consistent practice of explaining and arguing the necessity to replace capitalism by socialism—in the party's faith that a majority of industrial workers and farmers could understand and join in a movement for a society in which production would be controlled by those who did the work. Socialists believed that the trade unions were the economic arm of the working class and the party was the political arm. But they limited the meaning of "political" to electoral activity and tended to limit Socialist activity in the unions to getting the workers to vote Socialist (although Socialists in the AFL did stand for and often agitated for industrial unionism).

In accordance with this political perspective, the party was organized along the lines of electoral subdivisions and allowed substantial participation and initiative by the membership. There were forty-eight state parties, each with a good deal of autonomy from the national organization. Each city constituted a local, with branches that corresponded to ward or other political subdivision lines. Party officers were elected at local, state, and national conventions, and party programs and policies were subject to approval by membership referendum. In addition, a small number of locals could initiate policy proposals and the recall of elected officers. The foreign-language federations, made up of Socialists from various European countries, were semi-autonomous. They had their own locals and press and were represented in the national office by translator-secretaries.

Although this structure did not fit a politics based on the Russian experience, the Communist parties did not immediately change the form of organization inherited from the Socialist Party in 1919. The Communist Labor Party made no changes; the Communist Party added shop nuclei (branches based on the place of work) to the geographical branches. While the parties were "underground" they adopted some Russian forms, but with the founding of the Workers Party in late 1921 both Communist parties came together in an organization that closely resembled the old Socialist Party.

By mid-1924 the American party came under increasing pressure to "Bolshevize" itself, which meant a change both in policy and in organization. In part, Bolshevization was designed to bring the American party into closer touch with industrial workers by establishing factory branches and setting up "fractions" in non-party organizations. (Fractions were party caucuses that operated secretly and had no authority to make policy for themselves.) These changes meant abstention from electoral politics and a shift into the factories and unions, where the fractions operated. The policy of getting into closer contact with workers within major industries, and of de-emphasizing alliances with leaders of electoral parties, prepared the Communist Party for its role in the late 1930s as organizers for John L. Lewis and the CIO. But Bolshevization also strengthened the syndicalist tendencies within the Communist Party. Factory cells and concentration on trade union work tended to function as a substitute for public activity directed at winning state power. The Communist Party did agitate for its version of socialism until the mid-1930s, as we will see, but it did so in a manner that mystified the idea of socialism and made it more and more abstract.

From 1924, when Stalin replaced Lenin as the leader of the Russian party, developments in the American party became a grotesque shadow of the struggles within the Soviet Union. Intense factionalism characterized these years, with a "right" turn when Stalin was defeating Trotsky and Zinoviev, and then a "left" turn in 1927 when he was eliminating Bukharin. This "left" turn, which lasted until the adoption of the Popular Front policy in 1935, was known as the Third Period. In Russia this was the period when rapid industrialization and the collectivization of agriculture began. In the rest of the world, on instructions from the International, Communist parties broke with all liberal and socialist movements and attempted to build their own unions and reform organizations. During the early part of the Third Period, factions continued within the Communist parties around the world. But in the middle of the Third Period, after Stalin emerged victorious and without rivals in Russia, the other Communist parties quickly eliminated any overt signs of factionalism. Thereafter the Communists had a new understanding of "monolithism," in which the absence of factions accurately reflected the state of things in the Soviet Union.

The results of the Third Period were bad throughout the world. In China the Third Period followed, and may have been partly influenced by, the collapse of the Comintern alliance with Chiang Kai-shek, whose Kuomintang sat as a fraternal party on the executive committee of the International in the mid-1920s. After Chiang broke with the Communists in 1927 and almost destroyed the Chinese party, Stalin pressured the Communists into staging the disastrous uprising in Canton. Similarly, in Europe, the International began insisting in 1928 that Italian fascism was about to collapse of its own internal contradictions and that it would be followed by a revolutionary upsurge and Communist victory. Antonio Gramsci opposed this view in prison, but the Comintern imposed it on the Italian party,[20] just as it later pressured the German party to adopt the view that Hitler's rise to power was ephemeral, merely a prelude to proletarian revolution.[21] The German slogan was *"Nach Hitler uns"* ("After Hitler us").

In the United States the effects of the Third Period were less disastrous than in Europe only because there was much less at stake. The party had succeeded briefly in breaking out of its isolation in 1924, when it participated in the attempt to form a Farmer-Labor Party along with other left-wing unionists in Minnesota and elsewhere. This experience had ended in disaster partly because Robert M. La Follette opposed forming a third party. He preferred to run for the presidency as an independent and needed the endorsement of the AFL—and part of the price of that endorsement was a denunciation of the Communists. But even if they had not been attacked by La Follette, the Communists would have destroyed their alliance with the Farmer-Laborites because their earlier policy of cooperation was denounced by the International as an impermissible "united front at the top." This made it necessary for the party to reverse virtually overnight its policy of the preceding six months and to sever its ties to the Farmer-Labor movement.[22]

[20] See Giuseppe Fiori, *Antonio Gramsci* (New York, 1971), pp. 249–258.

[21] See Isaac Deutscher, *The Prophet Outcast* (New York, 1963), pp. 131 ff.

[22] For a detailed account see Weinstein, *Decline,* pp. 313–323.

After the break with the Farmer-Laborites in 1924, the party was increasingly isolated from other socialist and left-liberal groups. In the next few years membership declined, in the face of Bolshevization, from about 16,000 in the beginning of 1925 to 9,500 at the end of the 1920s.[23] During these years, Communists were active in the shops and in several unions, but their trade union policies were unclear. William Z. Foster, in keeping with a lifelong commitment to working within the mainstream of the labor movement, consistently opposed dual unionism before the Third Period began. But other party members, with erratic support from Comintern leaders, sometimes violated Foster's strategy. The view of Socialists and AFL leaders simply as capitalist lackeys reinforced these tendencies, as did pronouncements from Moscow by A. Lozofsky, chief of the International's trade union division, about the danger of "overevaluation of the importance of the Fascist AFL." [24]

The outstanding example of Communist trade union activity during the mid-1920s was the Passaic textile strike of 1926. The strike took place in an ambiguous context within the party. In 1925 the Communist convention had urged the unionization of textile workers by "strengthening the existing organizations and the creation of new unions where none exist." This formulation could be understood in different ways, depending on one's view of dual unionism, and this became clear, with unfortunate results, in Passaic.

The United Textile Workers, the AFL union, had never tried to organize the Passaic mills. The IWW had conducted a long strike in 1913, just after their great victory at Lawrence, but had failed. In September 1925 the Botany Mill announced a 10 percent wage cut and other mills quickly followed suit. This spelled disaster for thousands of workers, half of whom were immigrant women earning less than $15 per week. It also spelled opportunity for the party and its policy of organizing textile workers.

Except for the results, the Passaic strike in 1926 was very much like the Lawrence textile strike of 1912. Like Lawrence, Passaic was a

[23] See Theodore Draper, *American Communism and Soviet Russia* (New York, 1960), p. 187.

[24] See A. Lozofsky, "Results and Prospects of the United Front," *The Communist International,* March 15, 1928, p. 146, cited in Draper, *American Communism and Soviet Russia,* p. 290.

mill town with thousands of immigrant workers of different nationalities. Women made up most of the work force. Wages were low and the AFL union was disinterested. The situation was desperate and the workers were ready to accept leadership from any experienced organizers. Like the IWW, which had a small local in Lawrence before the strike, the party had a small shop nucleus in Passaic, and, like the IWW, it had talented organizers available to press into service.

The main vehicle of party organizing at this time was its United Front committees. The original purpose of these committees was to agitate for unification of the various textile unions (there were some sixteen in all), but they also were available to serve as independent organizing groups. When the wage cuts hit Passaic, a local party member, Albert Weisbord, was assigned to set up a United Front Committee there. Weisbord, a young Harvard graduate, had joined the Communist Party after reading Lenin and then gone to work in a silk mill in Paterson, New Jersey. He issued membership books and dues stamps in the name of the United Front Committee as if it were itself a union. This, in turn, was opposed by the Foster faction within the party as dual unionism, and after some discussion it was agreed that Weisbord should stop issuing books and should affiliate his committee with an existing textile union.

Meanwhile, after feverish preparation, the Passaic strike started in January 1925. Some 5,000 Botany Mill employees and 11,000 from other mills walked out. The mill owners persuaded the city to put a Civil War Riot Act into effect and hundreds of workers were arrested. Police clubbed strikers, newspapermen, press photographers, and others friendly to the strikers, causing a national scandal and gaining the strikers much liberal sympathy and support. But the strike dragged on and on, opposed by a wide array of politicians and government officials, including the Secretary of Labor, by the press, and by the AFL as a whole (including the United Textile Workers). The strikers had little chance. Open leadership by the Communists made things worse, of course, and the ambivalence of party leadership confused the situation. Finally, in September, nine months after the strike started, the party decided that a settlement could not be reached under its leadership. The only solution was to offer the strike and the strikers to the UTW. After much negotiating, the AFL union agreed to take over the strike, but only if Weisbord and other known Communists left Passaic. That was agreed. The UTW took over. The strike dragged on for a while and was finally settled with no gains for the workers.

The Passaic strike was disposed of by turning it over to the AFL. This solution left Communist trade union policy somewhat unclear, since the major part of the strike was conducted openly under Communist leadership, while the "existing union" (the UTW) was brought in only at the end. Even so, the experience of the strike—the extreme difficulty Communists faced in leading strikes in open opposition not only to employers and the state, but also to existing trade union organizations—strengthened the anti-dual union tendencies within the party.

Unfortunately, the question of dual unionism was tied intimately to broader policy questions and, like these, was to be decided not by experience but by the needs of the Communist Party of the Soviet Union. When A. Lozofsky wrote in *The Communist International,* the Comintern's semi-monthly publication, that the Americans must stop "dancing a quadrille the whole time around the AFL and its various unions," the question was settled in the American party. Instead of courting the AFL, Lozofsky concluded, the party must "form unions in all those branches of industry where there is either no organization or where what exists is practically negligible." [25]

Except in the fur industry, where the Communists had gained control of the union under the leadership of Ben Gold, the new policy of dual unionism further isolated the party from organized labor. The effects were most negative in the industries that were relatively well organized and were outside of New York (where the Communists had their greatest strength among the needle trades workers).

The new policy had its worst effect in relation to the United Mine Workers of America, which was singled out for special mention at the Fourth Congress of the Red International of Labor Unions (known as the Profintern). "The organization of the Left Wing in the UMW and amongst unorganized miners," the Profintern resolution stated, "must prepare to become the basis of a new union." [26] This spelled disaster for the Communists who had been working in the UMW in a coalition to overthrow John L. Lewis.

In 1926 John Brophy led a challenge to John L. Lewis's control of

[25] Lozofsky, *ibid.*
[26] Quoted in Draper, *American Communism and Soviet Russia,* p. 289.

the UMW. Although Brophy, a former Socialist, was defeated in his attempt to win the presidency of the union, the "save the union" committee that he organized continued as an anti-administration coalition of leftists and dissidents. The main strength of the committee was in Illinois (District 12 of the UMW) and in Kansas (District 14). The Communists, who had helped organize the "save the union" committee through their Trade Union Educational League (TUEL), worked closely with Brophy, Alex Howat of Kansas, and the leaders of the Illinois district. In 1927 and early 1928 the UMW suffered serious losses as a result of overproduction of coal, increasing competition from non-union southern mines, and the determination of the major northern companies to eliminate the competitive disadvantage of paying union wages under such conditions. As conditions worsened, particularly after the major strike in 1927 was lost, the "save the union" committee made headway. But just as it did (in late 1928), the Profintern issued its instruction that Communists in the UMW had to become the basis of a new union.

To the non-Communist leaders of the "save the union" committee this new policy was incomprehensible, particularly since it flew in the face of Foster's lifelong opposition to dual unionism. He had joined the party only after it had adopted a policy of "boring from within" the existing unions in 1921—and the "save the union" committee was his most successful venture in the 1920s, one that Foster spent five months helping to organize. Yet in the summer of 1928, only months after Pat Toohey, a leading Communist miner, had joined Brophy and Powers Hapgood in calling a "save the union" conference, Foster issued a call for a new miners union (the National Miners Union). Hapgood could not understand this about-face and went to Foster to plead with him to stand by his lifelong opposition to dual unions. Foster could only reply: "Powers, the Communist Party decided that policy. As a good Communist, I just have to go along." [27] True to his word, Foster organized the National Miners Union and split the progressive opposition forces in the UMW, thus assuring Lewis's continued control.

The Theory and Practice of The Third Period

The results of the Third Period were horrendous, especially given the opportunities for the growth of a socialist movement created by the

---

[27] From an interview of Hapgood by Saul Alinsky, quoted in Alinsky's *John L. Lewis* (New York, 1970), p. 58.

crash and the onset of the Great Depression in 1929. And the politics of the Third Period did not have its origin in changing conditions in the world as a whole, but was imposed on the world Communist movement by the Russian party in line with its domestic policies—its determination to embark on a program of forced industrialization through a series of five-year plans. Nevertheless, the Russian Socialists had succeeded in taking power and they were living in the real world. Their understanding of the nature of world capitalism and of the revolutionary process, while certainly not immediately transferable to the already industrialized nations, still had something to teach Socialists in the United States and elsewhere. And the strong appeal of the Communist Party for revolutionaries in the West, although influenced by the fact that the Communist Party was the recognized party of the Bolsheviks, was in part a result of Lenin's ideas about the state and the role of the party in leading a revolutionary struggle. Communist ideas, therefore, cannot simply be dismissed as mindless reflexes of the Kremlin line, however much this has been true or appeared to be true over most of the party's existence. The party was made up of real human beings. Their ideas were shaped by their own experience and by the experience of the American left—particularly of the Socialist Party and the IWW—as much as by their relationship to the Comintern. And more important, the major ideas of the Communist Party affected the course of events in the United States from the late 1920s through the 1940s and continue to influence the thinking and politics of thousands of American Socialists who have never had any direct organizational ties to the party. It is, therefore, important to look at the writings of the party's most authoritative spokesman during the Third Period to understand its ability to remain at the center of socialist politics in the United States during these years and its inability to build a mass movement for socialism in the years of the obvious collapse of American capitalism. This is particularly important because the ideas and politics of the Third Period remained the basic ideas of party members throughout the later periods of the Popular Front and the post-World War II years. The main difference was that during the Third Period the private and public ideas of Communists tended to be the same, while in later years the Third Period ideas were held in private behind a façade of militant liberalism.

Fortunately, William Z. Foster laid out the politics and theory of the Third Period in 1932. Called *Toward Soviet America,* Foster's book is designed to explain the decline of capitalism, the rise of socialism, and the revolutionary way out of the crisis under the leadership of the Communist Party. During the Third Period, the party's main theoretical assumption was that capitalism was in a general state of collapse and would be unable to solve its problems (by which it was meant that capitalism would be unable to reestablish social stability). Socialism was central to Communist politics at this time, and capitalism in crisis was continually compared to the growth of socialism in the Soviet Union. Thus, Foster wrote that "the masses of toilers suffering under the burdens of crisis" were "keenly discontented" and wanted to "find a way out of their intolerable situation." [28]

Their growing realization of capitalism's inability to provide security and a decent living was "further strengthened" by "the spectacular rise of socialism in the Soviet Union." And the Communists' important message for the human race was to spread the word about socialism as revealed in Russia. But, Foster insists, "Capitalism is deeply anxious that the masses do not get this message." Accordingly, "from the outset it has carried on a campaign of falsification of the Russian Revolution entirely without parallel in history." There had been "a veritable ocean of lies in the capitalist press against the U.S.S.R." Nor were the commercial papers and major party politicians the only ones who had conducted this campaign. The AFL and the Socialist Party, both "defenders of the capitalist system, have outdone even the capitalists themselves in this wholesale vilification." These misrepresentations demanded a reply, which was the purpose of the book.

This equation of socialism with the process of development in the Soviet Union runs throughout Foster's argument and must be kept in mind in order to understand Communist thinking, at least until 1956. In 1932, of course, the policies and events (the purge trials, the Nazi-Soviet pact, the assassination of Trotsky) that gave Stalin and Stalinism its chilling connotations had not yet occurred, and Foster's characterization of the capitalist campaign of villification against the Russian Revolution was largely accurate. Yet, if the capitalists, the AFL leaders, and, to a much lesser degree, the Socialists slandered the Rus-

[28] William Z. Foster, *Toward Soviet America* (New York, 1932), preface.

sians, Foster did the opposite. He set the Soviet Union up as a model, ripped out of its own historical context, to be copied and used as an absolute basis of comparison. This, despite the fact that in 1932 the Soviet Union was only beginning to industrialize, the great majority of the population were still illiterate peasants, starvation was still widespread, and conditions of work and the standard of living were still extremely poor in comparison with that of American workers.

Despite this, in the first chapter, on the decline of capitalism, Foster wrote that the "most striking and significant political and social fact in the world today" was the "glaring contrast between the industrial, political, and social conditions prevailing in the capitalist countries and those obtaining in the Soviet Union." He then went on to recount the paralysis in the capitalist nations. Unemployment and destitution are the lot of masses of workers. War is "already here in Manchuria" and preparations for future wars go on, on an unprecedented scale. Fascist terrorism is spreading, alongside increasing revolutionary struggle by the working and farming masses. On the other hand, Russian industry and agriculture were "expanding at an unheard-of rate, the Soviet Union being the only country in the world not prostrated by the economic crisis." There, the masses were all employed, standards of living were rapidly rising, and they were "building a new and free proletarian democracy." In short, as capitalism goes down, the Soviet Union "forges ahead faster and faster on every front."

Again, there was a good deal of truth in this description as long as it was taken as a characterization of a process going on in two historically very different contexts—as long, that is, as it was not taken literally. But to Foster, and to Communists in general at that time, the "Rise of Socialism" was synonymous not only with the existence of the Soviet Union—with the fact of the Revolution—but also with social conditions there. The Soviet Union, Foster wrote, was "showing in the everyday demonstration of life its immense superiority in every field over the obsolete capitalist system. The very existence of the Soviet Union has a profoundly revolutionary effect upon the working class." [29] And the Soviets "open the door to an era of general prosperity, freedom, and cultural advance hitherto completely unknown to the world." [30] This

[29] *Ibid.*, p. 71.
[30] *Ibid.*, p. 72.

was shown not only in the statistics for increasing production in Russia (which were impressive as indicators of growth but puny when compared to the level of production in the United States even in the midst of the Depression), but also in Russia's "cultural revolution." Public schooling was now compulsory and illiteracy was being wiped out in the industrial centers and would "also soon go from the villages." But more than that, the Russian Revolution was seen as "giving the greatest stimulation to science, literature, music, the theatre, etc., that the world has ever known." [31]

This vision of the Soviet Union was closely related to the idea that the Communist parties, affiliated with the Third International, were the only true bearers of socialism and that all other parties and groups were either fakers or worse. Conditions in the United States were rapidly freeing workers "from the illusion that capitalism provides the way to prosperity," Foster wrote. Soon, "under the banner of the Communist International," the workers would have a revolutionary organization and program, and then they would "break through the Social-Fascist trickery and violence with which decadent capitalism sustains itself." Capitalism, he concluded, was "heading irresistibly toward proletarian revolution." [32]

The Third Period line, reflected especially in the attitude of the International to German fascism, was that capitalism was in precipitous decline and the the main danger lay in underestimating the potential for working-class revolutionary action. As Foster wrote, the Depression was "not just another crisis" but was part of "a rapidly deepening general crisis of capitalism," which was "setting on foot forces that are drastically undermining the very economic, political, and social foundations of capitalism, and hastening that system ever faster toward proletarian revolution." In retrospect, that looks more like self-hypnosis than a sober analysis of American society. But at the time, both within the United States and in Europe, the description appeared reasonable. And if there had been a socialist party capable of posing the question of socialism in terms appropriate to conditions in the United States, Foster's view might not have been as far off as it now appears.

Communist theory about "the conquest of political power," that

[31] *Ibid.*, p. 109.
[32] *Ibid.*, p. 70.

is, how the Revolution will occur, has always been weakest on the question of socialist consciousness within the working class—how the masses would come to understand the need for socialism. This is probably because the Bolsheviks faced a different problem in gaining power in Russia, and the party has never been able to develop theory on its own. But Communist understanding of the lessons learned by the Bolsheviks was solid. Even though Foster could lapse into talk about the inevitability of proletarian revolution, he also understood that capitalism would never completely collapse of its own weight. There would never be an "absence of a way out" for the bourgeoisie, Foster wrote, "until it faces the revolutionary armed proletariat." Civil war will be necessary not because the workers want it that way, but "because the ruling class will never permit itself to be ousted without such a fight." He then quoted the *Program of the Communist International:* "The conquest of power by the proletariat does not mean peacefully 'capturing' the ready-made bourgeois State machinery by means of a parliamentary majority." [33]

"The Social Fascists," Foster went on, "make a great parade of their theory of the "gradual evolution of capitalism into Socialism through a process of peaceful parliamentarism." Morris Hillquit, for example, argued that in the more developed capitalist nations, "the necessary transitional forms, or at least a large part of them," might be "gradually conquered through the direct control by the proletariat of important organs of the state, such as municipalities or legislatures, or through the indirect influence of the growing labor movement." To Hillquit, Foster charged, this meant that the "present imperialist government is actually the 'Socialist transitional State.'" [34]

But if the socialists did have a gradualist approach to revolution, Foster had a hazy conception of a mediation between day-to-day struggles and the seizure of power. Reform did not necessarily weaken capitalist hegemony and was not necessarily a step toward socialism, of course. As Foster pointed out, reforms had traditionally been used to strengthen the existing system and to secure the loyalty of working people to the corporations and capitalist society—as the corporate liberals

[33] *Ibid.,* p. 214.
[34] *Ibid.,* pp. 214–215.

in the New Deal would soon brilliantly demonstrate. But if socialists abstained from participation in reform movements, if they did not attempt to create transitional forms that could embody socialist principles and make possible a continuous struggle for working-class control of social institutions, they would inevitably remove themselves from meaningful participation in the political life of society. As Foster's book makes clear, the refusal to take political reform seriously left the Communist Party with only an abstract appeal to socialism—"the Soviet Union now forecasts the general outlines of the new social order . . ." [35]—combined with a syndicalist day-to-day practice.

Foster generalized this view in this way: the workers, he wrote, "will carry out a militant policy now in defense of their daily interests and, finally, following the example of the Russian workers, they will abolish capitalism and establish Socialism." [36] In accordance with this scenario—by which struggles around the immediate needs of workers on the job are somehow transformed into revolutionary consciousness and the need for a Soviet America—the Communist Party based its work "directly upon the mills, mines, and factories." Its principle, Foster insisted, was "to make every shop a fortress for Communism" by following "closely the life of the workers in the industries" and by "adapting its immediate program of struggle to their needs." Organizationally, this meant that instead of being based on territorial branches, as the Socialist Party was, the Communist Party had the shop nucleus as its basic unit. This form of organization, along with the party's overall strategy, strengthened the syndicalist tendencies among Communists, particularly in the Foster wing of the party.

Party culture, the glorification of the worker as worker, the development of "proletarian" literature, the vision of the factory as the center of future social life, were parts of this syndicalist tendency, at once being strengthened by it and reinforcing it. And, of course, the proletarian cult was bolstered by the Russians and by Russian literature and films. This was so because the Soviets were moving millions of people into industry during these years and it was necessary for them to emphasize all the positive aspects of proletarianization, to put the

[35] *Ibid.*, p. 268.
[36] *Ibid.*, p. 212.

highest possible value on the factory worker in order to encourage the rural population to take up jobs in industry with a minimum of resistance.

In the United States this orientation would be immediately useful during the 1930s because the major social issue during these years was the creation of an industrially organized trade union movement, the Congress of Industrial Organizations (CIO). The party's syndicalist orientation, and its members' actual experience in organizing independent (Communist) unions during the Third Period, would prove useful both to the organizers of the CIO and to the party in gaining a substantial foothold within the CIO. But in the long run, this orientation did much more harm than good to the party and to the cause of socialism.

It did so for two reasons. First, the emphasis on shop work and building unions also meant an emphasis on industrial workers as an interest group within class society and a de-emphasis on the working class as a potential universal class capable of running society as a whole. This approach tended to perpetuate the fragmentation of working people that was imposed on them by capitalism. To think about socialism and a socialist movement as if it were simply concerned with workers' control over immediate goods production encouraged a lack of concern about other aspects of society, about the need for a socialist politics in other spheres of social life. During the Third Period this made it easier for the party's appeals to socialism to remain abstract and subordinate to immediate defensive activity in the factories. Later, in the Popular Front Period, it made it easier for the party to support liberal New Dealers as long as they were pro-union and to forget altogether the need for a popular socialist consciousness.

The party's syndicalist tendency also led to an emphasis on the industrial workers as a vanguard class that was strategically placed to shut society down and to an underemphasis of the proletariat as a universal class, that has within it the ability to run society. Marx's idea that the working class would be the first class in history whose victory would mean the end of class society was based on this: that as capitalism developed, the working class would come to include within itself all the skills and knowledge necessary for running society as a whole. It could thus speak truly in the interest of all of humanity—at least so long as the workers understood that socialism meant the end of involuntary divisions of labor imposed by class society. Again, the Communists' relationship to the Soviets undermined Marx's conception of the proletariat as a universal class. For reasons that we have already seen, the working class in Russia did not yet have the potential to be a universal class. The situation was different in the United States, but since the conception of socialism put forth by the party was based on the Soviet model, the party's emphasis was put on workers as workers and not on workers as potentially self-governing citizens. Thus, for example, Foster's view of a socialist America stressed the need to further concentrate and centralize industry. And Foster stressed the need for scientific coordination and consolidation of industries, for their organization under a supreme central planning agency.

And what about democracy? How would the masses participate in self-government? Foster's answer was true to his syndicalist tendencies and consistent with Soviet reality at its best. The trade unions were to "draw the masses directly into the work of Socialist construction." They attended to "the protection of the immediate needs of the workers" (as they do in capitalist society). No important activities were "embarked upon without their consent" (which, of course, was not true under capitalist society). No labor law could go into effect without trade union consent and cooperation, and their "representatives occupy key positions in every stage of the economic and social organization." [37] Mass participation, then, was seen by Foster as the right to participate in defensive organizations with a veto power over plans made by other groups. As under capitalism, the unions spoke in the interest of workers as workers—for their immediate interests on the job. Although the unions were the mass organizations of the workers, they did "not, of themselves, actually lead the production, this being the task of the governmental economic organs" (in bourgeois society, of the capitalist class, in Russia of the party). In other words, Foster's view of socialism left the workers organized only to defend their immediate interests as workers, while basic social priorities and the decisions of society as a whole were left to the Communist Party.

Once again, this view threw together a syndicalist practice with an anti-historical acceptance of the developing state socialism of the So-

[37] *Ibid.*, p. 219.

viets. "The American Soviet government," Foster wrote, would "be organized along the broad lines of the Russian Soviets." [38] Assuming the best of intentions on the part of the Communists, this would mean that social priorities and the allocation of resources would be decided in the interest of the working population (as contrasted to capitalism, where these decisions are made on the basis of maximizing profit for privately-owned corporations). But it did not mean that these decisions would be made by the workers. At best, it would mean a benevolent paternalism, in which the workers would be permanently infantilized. This was so because, under the Soviet form of government as put forth by Foster, even the forms of democratic rights known under capitalism would be denied. Under what Foster called the dictatorship of the proletariat, "all capitalist parties—Republican, Democratic, Progressive, Socialist, etc.—will be liquidated, the Communist Party functioning alone as the Party of the toiling masses." This Foster understood as "the birth of real democracy."

Foster did recognize that as a "highly industrialized country" the United States already had the industrial bases for socialism and that the primary problem facing the workers was "to get the political power." This contrasted with the Soviets, where the Communists "not only had to conquer power but also had to build a great industrial system." In contrast, socialism in the United States could be achieved with "the present American industrial technique plus Soviets." [39] But in Russia the dictatorship of the proletariat, at best, meant the dictatorship of a small minority, since the working class comprised a distinct minority of the population. And in practice, of course, the dictatorship was of the party, not the class. In the United States a dictatorship of the proletariat would have to mean the dictatorship of the great majority, since by Foster's own estimate, the working class comprised 70 percent of the population at that time.

In several ways the Revolution in Russia did mean a real advance in democracy, and this the socialists and others either underestimated or denied. Legal trade unions were in themselves a great advance over czarism. The elimination of illiteracy was another, and a necessary,

[38] *Ibid.*, pp. 271–272.
[39] *Ibid.*, p. 270.

prerequisite to participation by workers and peasants in modern social and political life. And the rapid development of industry under the five-year plans would bring tremendous improvements in the everyday life of Russian working people. But the American working class was already literate, already had a level of living that the Russians would not achieve until after World War II, and also had the legal right to form trade unions (although they did not already have a substantial trade union movement). And they also already had long been accustomed to the formal democratic rights of liberal capitalist society. For American working people real democracy had to mean more than the simple elimination of the Republican and Democratic parties, controlled as they were by the corporations. It had to mean participation as equals in all processes of social decision-making. This implied an open political system, decentralization of decision-making and administration, and access to participation in all aspects of social planning for all working people. To American workers, Foster's formula appeared simply as the replacement of the disguised class rule of capitalism by the rule of an open elite under "socialism." This appearance was, of course, strengthened by Foster's own formulation, which lumped both the Progressives and the Socialists as capitalist parties, implying thereby that there could only be one tendency within socialism, and that public life and social decision-making would be the monopoly of that tendency. Small wonder that the Communists did not succeed in making their vision of socialism widely popular, that they could not make the question of socialism versus capitalism a genuine public issue during the years that they did openly espouse a socialist politics.

But, during the Third Period, the party did try. It was, after all, the party of Lenin, and to the best of its ability, and within the constraints placed upon it by the International, it did attempt to develop a socialist, as opposed to a syndicalist, politics. Therefore, as Foster pointed out, the party practiced "revolutionary parliamentarism." This meant placing candidates during elections and making "every effort to elect them." It combined "parliamentary action inside legislative bodies with its mass action outside"; and it fought to "force all possible concessions from the government." [40] But, possibly because the party had

[40] *Ibid.*, p. 255.

so little success in arousing popular support for its version of socialism, and also because its model of revolution was based on the Bolshevik insurrection, its main approach to parliamentary work was to use it negatively. This meant using ''public forums to expose the capitalist character of the government,'' making ''clear to workers that the capitalist democracy is a sham,'' and stressing that ''there must be no illusions about peacefully capturing the State for the working class.''

Unfortunately, this approach to parliamentary activity created a psychology that saw not only that capitalist democracy was a sham, but also that electoral activity was itself a sham, except when conducted for the purpose of exposing those in power. Communist electoral work was not seen as part of a process of taking power. This took place entirely outside of the existing political process in the party's view. Taking power meant either a general strike or some other form of insurrection. It did not mean working through the electoral process, as well as outside, to build a majority for socialism. The knowledge that the ruling class would not likely give up its power simply because it lost an election, that it would be necessary to disarm the capitalist class by dismantling its state apparatus (including the army and the police), led the party to see serious long-term participation in the electoral arena as at best useless. But this meant that the party excluded itself from the real arena of politics within liberal capitalist society—the electoral arena, which was the only avenue to power available to working people, and the one through which the capitalists continuously legitimated their own rule. As long as the parliamentary route was available, a party that did not attempt to gain power through it, no matter how well it understood the limitations of such a path, could not be taken seriously by the majority of the population.

What, then, were the party's accomplishments during the Third Period? In the light of the possibilities created by the crash of 1929, they were substantially less than the accomplishments of the old Socialist Party during and before World War I. Yet party activity, especially in trying to build Communist unions, did prepare them for their role as organizers of the CIO during the New Deal. The party had built a new organization; it had eliminated outward manifestations of political tendencies, which was at least as much a liability as an asset, but which did permit Communists to throw all their energies into projects and give them an immediate practical effectiveness. In the Third Period their main project was to build industrial unions in the basic industries. This they did with energy and determination but with very meager results. Nevertheless, when this experience was put to use within the framework of John L. Lewis's Committee for Industrial Organization, the results would be impressive.

The party did work hard during the Third Period to build its unions and to build the party itself. And there was a social basis for building mass unions and for socialism. Its experience was not that it could not move people to action or recruit members, but that its actions almost uniformly failed and its recruits did not last long. For example, the party's National Miners Union conducted a strike of coal miners in the Pennsylvania–West Virginia–Eastern Ohio region in the summer of 1931. This was the NMU's biggest effort, although another strike, in Harlan, Kentucky, was better known and had firmer support from the local miners. When the strike began, the NMU had about 100 members. During the strike it signed up 25,000, and the party itself recruited 1,000 new members. In addition, the strike enabled the party, for the first time, to come out with its own candidates in local municipal elections in the strike area, and a Communist was elected to local office.[41]

The party carried on mass actions in an attempt to win popular support: hunger marches to Washington and Pittsburgh, mass demonstrations of strikers at Harrisburg and Washington, an anti-war demonstration on August 1. But the party was using these demonstrations as much to fight the United Mine Workers of America (led by John L. Lewis) and the Socialist Party as it was to win the miners' grievances. Unity of union and leftist forces around the immediate issues was the furthest thing from the Communists' purpose. Making the strike "political" meant "mass propaganda" not only "for political demands against the police," but also "against the deceptive contracts concluded between the employers and the U.M.W.A. fakers." Trying to make the strikers "understand the role of the Communist Party, its aims and methods of struggle," the party undertook "several political steps toward combating the Socialist Party." In the end, with active hostility

---

[41] S. Wilner, "Some Lessons from the Latest Strike," *The Communist International,* vol. IX, no. 2 (February 1, 1932), pp. 60 ff.

from the UMWA, and without support even from other left-wing groups, the strike failed and NMU membership melted away. In all, these activities brought 11,000 new members into the party in 1931, but 7,477 of these quit in the same period.[42] Even so, because of the desperate conditions of the Depression and the party's militant activities, it did have a sizable net gain of membership between 1929 and 1935.

[42] *Ibid.,* p. 61; *The Communist International,* vol. IX, no. 15 (August 15, 1932), p. 516.

3/

THE POPULAR FRONT

Building the CIO

The Third Period ended following Hitler's annihilation of the German Communists and Social Democrats. In line with the International's Third Period views and with its explicit support, the German party had viewed Hitler as ephemeral. But Hitler quickly destroyed the organized socialist movement—and consolidated his power—by imprisoning or murdering Communist leaders. The Russians, belatedly realizing that Nazism was a formidable opponent and that Hitler's threats against world Communism menaced the future of the Soviet Union, now desperately sought to prevent the formation of a coalition of capitalist powers aimed at their destruction. The main priority became building alliances wherever possible in order to halt the growth of fascist power. The Third Period view that Social Democrats (progressives and liberals in the United States) were the main enemies (because they confused and misled the potentially revolutionary workers) had to be repudiated. Liberal forces now became precious defenders of democratic rights, which were upheld against fascist terror.

Thus, after 1935, these erstwhile ''social fascists'' became sought-after allies in a front of liberals and socialists to defend liberal (bourgeois) democracy against warlike and totalitarian reaction. This change in the Communist line was most strikingly evident in the change from the early days of Franklin D. Roosevelt's first administration. In those days, the Communists had attacked both the Agricultural Adjustment Act (AAA) and the National Recovery Act (NRA) as fascist legislation.[1] But after the Popular Front was proclaimed, the party attacked the Supreme Court as fascist for declaring these same acts unconstitutional. Similarly, during the National Miners Union days, John L. Lewis had been attacked as a bureaucratic leader of the "fascist AFL." Yet when Lewis set up the Committee for Industrial Organization within the AFL, and later led the CIO out of the AFL to found the Congress of Industrial Organizations as a rival federation, the Communists gradually gave him their full support (as any serious left movement would have been compelled to do). But they went even further: Communist organizers by the score went to work for Lewis entirely on his terms. They were *his* organizers, under his leadership. As Lewis's biographer, Saul Alinsky, observed, for more than six years "the Communists slavishly followed Lewis' line." [2] Their support ended only in June 1941 when the Nazis invaded the Soviet Union and the Communist Party switched to support Roosevelt's interventionist policy, while Lewis continued to oppose it. Earl Browder, party general secretary in the 1930s, went out of his way to emphasize this policy by attacking others on the left who gave critical support to the CIO. In a report to the plenary meeting of the Central Committee in June 1937, Browder singled out as a "horrible example of what we should avoid in the trade union line" a resolution adopted by the Massachusetts Socialist Party convention. The Massachusetts Socialists had warned against "reliance on the reactionary trade union bureaucracy" and cautioned that CIO officials could "not be relied upon to provide correct leadership for the progressive forces in the trade unions." Browder dismissed this as "sniping on non-essential questions." The Socialists' observation that it was "only an accident of history that John L. Lewis and his associ-

---

[1] There was a partial truth in this charge. The AAA and NRA were an advanced form of liberal corporatism. Fascism was a non-constitutional or totalitarian form of corporatism. In both cases the various class interests were balanced within the framework of preserving corporate capitalism; in the former this was done within the traditional constitutional framework, in the latter it was done by fiat.

[2] Saul Alinsky, *John L. Lewis* (New York, 1970), p. 154.

ates'' appeared as ''representatives of the progressive forces by advocating what are at present progressive policies,'' and that this situation was ''not at all permanent,'' earned Browder's scorn.[3]

The Popular Front period began in 1935. From then until 1939, when the Soviet Union signed a nonaggression pact with the Nazi government in Germany and the Second World War began, the liberal forces in the New Deal, as well as Socialists and independent radicals, were courted by the Communist Party. The Popular Front against fascism in Europe was an attempt at alliances of all groups that would defend constitutional government against fascist dictatorship. In the United States the Communists interpreted this to mean the Democrats and those on the left against the Republicans and the monopolies. Of course, the Republicans represented no greater threat to constitutional government in the United States than did the New Dealers—indeed, in many ways the Roosevelt administrations had more contempt for democratic procedures than did their Republican predecessors. And, as the Communists had insisted in 1933, the NRA and the AAA, although they were achieved within a constitutional regime, were nevertheless similar to the corporate statist ideas of Italian fascism. But if the Communists totally misunderstood and exaggerated the threat of fascism in the United States, the Popular Front was nevertheless popular. And it was tolerated by the New Dealers because it played into Roosevelt's strategy of labeling his opponents ''economic royalists'' and of smearing Huey Long and his share-the-wealth movement as ''fascist'' (a view supported by the party).

This aside, the party's success after 1935 can be attributed primarily to its trade union activity. Communists participated eagerly and selflessly in building the CIO. While new unions were rapidly organizing millions of workers in the mass production industries, the Communists were an important—and essential—part of the movement. They were prominent in many CIO unions and controlled several. This was especially true in the industries where the party had been active in the 1920s and early 1930s, first working in the AFL and then trying to build their own unions. For although the party was unable to build any substantial industrial unions of its own (except in the fur industry, where

---

[3] Earl Browder, *The People's Front* (New York, 1938), p. 178.

they gained control of an already existing union), it had established disciplined groups of dedicated and militant organizers. Within the unions they controlled, Communists were generally more militant than non-Communists, and they consistently supported the rights of black workers to union membership and more equal job opportunities. In general, also, they fought for and established more democratic unions than did the old trade union bureaucrats—although the differences were not always substantial.

The Communists played a central role in building the CIO for two reasons. First was their experience in trying to organize industrial unions under the auspices of the Trade Union Unity League (TUUL) between 1929 and 1934, and also their activity in the many Unemployed Councils, groups of unemployed workers, which they helped organize and lead in the early 1930s. Second was their reputation as opponents of the "moribund, craft-dominated" AFL bureaucracy, combined with their determination to work "responsibly" with these old-line leaders in order to promote labor unity—once the Third Period had ended. Their turnabout coincided perfectly, partly by luck but also partly as the result of experience, with the development of the CIO and Lewis's determination to build a conservative industrial union movement.[4] Since Communists had been agitating for industrial unions for several years before Lewis emerged as the leader of the CIO, they had the ability to mobilize many militants in the shops who were still suspicious of Lewis and the other old-line leaders who dominated the CIO. This made Communists valuable organizers: they could go where United Mine Workers organizers could not, and they were willing to work hard and do what few old AFL organizers would do.[5]

In the early 1930s the Communists had built small unions in sev-

---

[4] Once the line changed on dual TUUL unions the Communists went back into the AFL and were determined not to cause further splits. Thus they reacted cautiously to the development of the CIO, working with it in the new unions but also being careful not to alienate the AFL. For a discussion that exaggerates this process (from an anti-Communist perspective), see Irving Howe and Lewis Coser, *The American Communist Party* (Boston, 1957), pp. 368–371.

[5] As Saul Alinsky observes in explaining why Lewis used Communists as organizers: "Every place where new industrial unions were being formed, young and middle-aged Communists were working tirelessly. . . . the Communists worked indefatigably, with no job being too menial or unimportant." Alinsky, *op. cit.,* p. 153.

eral key industries—coal mining, steel, automobile, and maritime. Party militants had worked hard and earned reputations as skilled and usually selfless organizers, but their activity was usually in competition with the bureaucratic skeletons of AFL unions and sometimes in direct struggle against the "social fascists" in the AFL. The potential of the TUUL was strictly limited both by its dual unionism and by its insistence on a "revolutionary" politics that exhorted American workers to follow "the path beaten out by the Russian workers" as the only hope for salvation.[6]

After the establishment of the National Recovery Administration, with Section 7a that granted workers the right to organize, the TUUL experienced some growth (to about 125,000 in 1934). But the AFL unions were growing much more rapidly. Despite this, in many industries the workers remained predominantly unorganized. As a result, a year or two before the change in line from the Third Period to the Popular Front, rank and file party unionists began to move back into the AFL. This was especially so in mining, where, as Earl Browder told the Communist International in 1934, "the reformist United Mine Workers swept through the coal fields with a broad recruitment campaign, and our Red Union members (without even consulting us) went along with the masses" into locals of the UMW.[7]

In the automobile industry in Cleveland a similar thing happened. Wyndham Mortimer, a sixteen-year veteran at the White Motor Company and a Communist,[8] began to organize a local of the Auto Workers Union (TUUL). Mortimer had solid support at White Motor and had signed up about half the workers when the AFL Metal Trades Council sent organizers to the plant (probably at the company's suggestion). The leaflet they distributed displayed an American flag and this message: "Join the bonafide AMERICAN labor union. Join the American Federation of Labor, the only union endorsed by our great President Franklin Delano Roosevelt." On the reverse side was what Mortimer called a "vicious attack on our independent union and the TUUL." This was

---

[6] Quoted in Murray Kempton, *Part of Our Time* (New York, 1955), p. 89.

[7] Browder speech to the executive committee of the Communist International, 13th Plenum, *The Communist International,* January 15, 1934. Quoted in Howe and Coser, *op. cit.,* p. 270.

[8] John Williamson, *Dangerous Scot* (New York, 1969), p. 101.

followed by a leaflet calling on White Motor workers to "Choose between Franklin Delano Roosevelt and Joe Stalin." [9]

In the face of this attack, Mortimer and his fellow workers concluded that it would be best to dissolve the TUUL local and to join the AFL Metal Trades Council federal local.[10] The AFL leaders weren't happy about this, but they had to accept the situation and try to control the local through their power to appoint its officers. Mortimer had joined the AFL not because he thought the TUUL was a mistake, but because it became clear to him that White Motor could use the TUUL to divide the workers. As a unionist, Mortimer's first principle was to achieve unity around the issues in the shop. Although he was a Communist, he understood that insisting on loyalty to the TUUL would lead only to confusion and divisions. He preferred to abandon the Auto Workers Union and fight it out within the AFL local for rank and file support and control.

Mortimer followed this policy in helping to set up the independent Cleveland District Auto Council, which the AFL executive council and the Metal Trades Council denounced as an outlaw. But because he had the full support of rank and file auto workers, he now refused to disband the Auto Council, even though it was not recognized by the AFL bureaucracy. The Cleveland District Auto Council was then used to help organize an industrial union in the automobile industry, which eventually became the United Automobile Workers Union when the CIO was formed.[11]

Mortimer acted on his own, and apparently with some opposition from party leaders,[12] but he was an exceptionally clear-thinking and independent person. In some industries, party policy was to reject any mergers or subordination of the TUUL unions. Thus, when a group of militant members of the AFL Amalgamated Association of Iron, Steel,

[9] Wyndham Mortimer, *Organize* (Boston, 1971), pp. 56–58.

[10] Federal unions were directly chartered by the AFL, but were not locals of affiliated international unions. They usually were temporary organizations whose members later were assigned to existing internationals in various trades.

[11] Mortimer, *op. cit.,* Chapters 5, 6, 7. See also Irving Bernstein, *Turbulent Years* (Boston), 1969, pp. 372–379.

[12] Mortimer, *ibid.,* p. 60. Mortimer writes about this incident as if the leader, Joe Zack (Kornfeder), opposed his move because he was a police agent at the time. Kornfeder was later expelled as an agent, but in this instance he was repeating the party line.

and Tin Workers tried to reorganize the Amalgamated along industrial lines, they were unable to get the kind of cooperation they needed from the TUUL union. The leaders of this group, all skilled steel workers from western Pennsylvania and eastern Ohio, had succeeded in building a rank and file majority within the Amalgamated but were unable to gain support from its leaders. At the Amalgamated convention in April 1934 the rank and filers forced through a resolution committing the union to demand recognition as an industrial union from the steel companies and for a strike in June if this demand was refused (as everyone knew it would be). But the small, weak Amalgamated did not have the resources to conduct a strike, and in any case the leaders had no intention of supporting one. Further, the leaders of the rank and file were inexperienced and had no national organization. In this situation, Clarence Irwin, a rank and file leader from Youngstown, decided to call on the Communists' Steel and Metal Workers Industrial Union (SMWIU) for aid.

The SMWIU had been founded almost two years earlier and had a membership of under 10,000. It had a small core of people—many of them former members of Unemployed Councils and now Communists—in a large number of mills. The SMWIU denounced the NRA as fascist and called on workers to rely on themselves rather than on the President or on the sell-out labor leaders in the AFL. By the time Irwin called on them for help, the SMWIU had conducted several bloody strikes and lost them all. After one of these, in Warren, Ohio, where many workers had been fired and the Finnish immigrant community (friendly to the Communists) had been driven from the city, the Communist Party local "was convinced of the impossibility [of organizing] independent labor unions in opposition to the old AFL." [13] The local sought to persuade William Z. Foster and other Communist leaders to abandon the policy of dual unionism in steel.

The rank and file movement offered the SMWIUers a perfect opportunity to overcome their isolation from AFL steelworkers, just as the SMWIU offered the rank and filers a national network of experienced

---

[13] Quoted by Staughton Lynd in an unpublished manuscript. The quote is from a speech by Leon Callow, former SMWIU organizer in Youngstown, Ohio, at Youngstown State University, April 14, 1972. This section on the SMWIU is taken largely from Lynd's account. See also Bernstein, *op. cit.,* pp. 197 ff.

organizers. But in May 1934 the Third Period had not yet been abandoned. Irwin wanted the SMWIU to give the rank and filers support and cooperation in the strike without any strings attached (a formal alliance with the SMWIU could only have meant expulsion of the rank and file group from the Amalgamated). Coordination at the local level and joint sponsorship of local meetings was all the rank and file could manage. This was turned down by the SMWIU, which insisted on a formal joint effort designed to give itself publicity and to be used by the Communists to build their own union.[14] Negotiations broke down, and the rank and file position in the Amalgamated was greatly weakened. By June, as a result of their own weakness and of maneuvers by AFL president William Green and administration leaders, the strike call was rescinded. Thereafter, until the passage of the Wagner Labor Relations Act and the formation of the CIO, some two years later, union organization in steel came virtually to a halt.

In the maritime industry the Communists also had a small but militant union, the Maritime Workers Industrial Union (MWIU). And, even before the adoption of the Popular Front, Communists were also active in the International Longshoremen's Association (ILA) and in the International Seamen's Union (ISU) on the West Coast. Before the establishment of the NRA and Section 7a, there were few union members among seamen on either coast. The ISU (AFL) had about 800 members, while the MWIU claimed more than 8,000 but probably had considerably fewer. But, as Murray Kempton observed, the precious few who joined the MWIU (and almost automatically passed over to the Communist Party) "were to be the fathers of a revolution" in the industry.[15] Among them were almost all the leaders who struggled to form the National Maritime Union of the CIO in 1937.

On occasion the MWIU succeeded in its activities, thus providing a glimpse of the later larger accomplishments to be made by the West Coast longshoremen and the National Maritime Union. Harry Alexander, a leader of the rank and file ISU group that created the NMU, was, with Joe Curran and Tom Ray, responsible for the Maritime Workers' greatest victory. In Baltimore in February 1934 he persuaded 700

[14] Lynd, *ibid.*
[15] Kempton, *op. cit.,* p. 90.

seamen to refuse to sign aboard any ship that would not hire through the union hiring hall he had set up. His Centralized Shipping Bureau, unique on the East Coast, admitted blacks and Filipinos as equals; the only test for shipping berths was length of time on the waiting list. The solidarity achieved in Baltimore made it possible to demand and get a $15 per month raise in wages (then between $50 and $60 per month). But because Baltimore was unique it was also vulnerable. The shipping companies began boycotting the port and starved out Alexander's experiment and with it the union hiring hall.[16]

A few months later the West Coast longshoremen's strike that led to the formation of the International Longshoremen's and Warehousemen's Union (ILWU/CIO)—and to the establishment of Harry Bridges as the major West Coast CIO leader—began. The Communists were to play a major role in the ILWU, largely because they had been instrumental in setting up the rank and file caucus in the old International Longshoremen's Association (ILA) in San Francisco. The MWIU began to organize San Francisco longshoremen in 1932 at the initiative of Harry Hynes, a Communist and West Coast MWIU organizer who was later killed in the Spanish Civil War. Hynes's first step was to launch the *Waterfront Worker*, a mimeographed (sometimes) monthly paper that was run off on a $5 mimeograph machine kept in his furnished room.[17] The paper, an instant success on the docks, presented the MWIU program and demands and attacked both the Blue Book, a company union on the waterfront, and the ILA and its president, Joe Ryan. The ILA had a dormant local in San Francisco—a remnant of a disastrous longshoremen's strike in 1919—and the Blue Book was thoroughly discredited on the docks, so the MWIU had reason to hope for success in building its own organization.

When Section 7a of the NRA regulations was enacted in the summer of 1933, the movement for a union on the waterfront blossomed. But it was the old ILA local, given fresh sanction by Joe Ryan, that came to life. As ILA buttons appeared all along the docks, the MWIU group, of which Harry Bridges was a member, joined it and formed a

---

[16] *Ibid.,* p. 91.

[17] Charles P. Larrowe, *Harry Bridges* (New York, 1972), Ch. 1; Al Richmond, *A Long View from the Left* (Boston, 1973), p. 216; Bernstein, *op. cit.,* pp. 259 ff. and 579. The following account is drawn largely from these three sources.

caucus known as Albion Hall, after the building in the Mission district where it held its meetings. The *Waterfront Worker,* with Bridges now an editor, became the voice of rank and file opposition within the San Francisco ILA. In the following months the ILA, constantly prodded by Bridges and the Albion Hall group (made up of Communists and independent radicals), tried to persuade the shipowners and stevedoring contractors to recognize the union. But the employers wanted no part of the ILA. Instead, they granted a 10-cent wage increase (bringing the basic wage to 85 cents an hour), incorporating it in an old agreement with the now moribund Blue Book.

This move by the employers increased the militancy of the longshoremen and their dissatisfaction with the timidity and ineffectiveness of the ILA local leadership. At a coast-wide convention of the ILA in February 1934, the Albion Hall group won a majority for its demands: abolition of the shape-up, establishment of a union hiring hall, and a wage increase to $1 an hour, a six-hour day, and a thirty-hour basic week. The employers were given until March 7 to accept. If they refused, a strike vote was to be taken and the strike begun on March 25.[18] This set the stage for the San Francisco general strike, which actually began on the evening of May 9, 1934, as a longshoremen's strike of all West Coast ports.

The next day, on May 10, the MWIU, with the largest membership of the seafaring unions, endorsed the ILA strike and went on strike themselves. Communist caucuses in shoreside AFL unions urged local support for the strike, and the party put the printing press of its *Western Worker* at the ILA's disposal when the union could not find commercial printers who would handle its strike bulletin. The party also helped in many other ways: It gathered food, supplied legal assistance, and provided large numbers of pickets from unemployed councils, the Workers' Ex-Servicemen's League, and other front groups.[19] MWIU support for the longshoremen forced the hand of ISU and other AFL unions, which soon after also went on strike—both in support of the ILA and to win recognition for themselves and a hiring hall for seamen. The strike was long and frequently bloody. Workers fought pitched battles with the police; strikers and non-strikers were killed; the city was

---

[18] Bernstein, *op. cit.,* p. 263.
[19] Larrowe, *op. cit.,* pp. 35–36.

virtually controlled by the striking workers for a short period. And in the end (the end of July 1934) the strike briefly became a general strike. This led to arbitration and a victory for the longshoremen, that included the establishment of a union-controlled hiring hall on the docks.

The San Francisco general strike changed the course of union development on the West Coast by establishing Bridges as a major power and by opening the AFL (and later the CIO) to Communist influence on a substantial scale. Similarly, on the East Coast, the strike changed the course of trade union development. Roused from its dormant state, the ISU, along with the licensed ships' officers and harbor workers, approached the shipowners to request negotiations. They were rebuffed. The MWIU then published a program similar to that of the West Coast ILA and engaged in several job actions. At that point, the ISU announced it was planning a strike, and the owners, feeling the reverberations from the West Coast, agreed to negotiate. The MWIU went ahead with a strike, which failed. And the shippers conferred nominal control of their crews on the ISU and agreed to a rate of $57.50 a month for seamen and union preference in hiring.

The result, as in the West, was to revive the old AFL union and cause the dissolution of the Communist union. The ISU quickly gained 13,000 members. Two months after the ISU contract was signed, the MWIU disbanded (February 1935) and its members were assigned to join the ISU as rank and filers. Tom Ray, a Communist who had been to Moscow as a delegate to the Profintern representing American seamen, began by putting out a mimeographed newspaper, the *ISU Pilot*. The *Pilot* held together a left within the ISU, but the Communists accomplished little in 1935 (they enlivened the normally soporific ISU meetings and led a short strike in Philadelphia). Then in February 1936 Joe Curran led the crew of the S.S. *California* in a refusal to cast off in San Pedro unless the company agreed to a $5 per month raise. Only after Secretary of Labor Frances Perkins personally promised to use her good offices to negotiate with the company did the crew go back to work. They then sailed to New York, where, upon landing, sixty-four of them were fired. In response, the men decided to call a general strike of seamen. But they didn't reckon with the ISU, which called them all Communists and expelled Ray, Curran, Alexander, and ten others.[20]

[20] Kempton, *op. cit.*, pp. 90–95.

Although some fifty ships were struck, the strike was soon beaten by the employers, with the help of Joe Ryan of the AFL longshoremen. As Ryan later explained, "We got some money from the shipowners. . . . We said 'Give us money; we are going to fight them.' We got the money and drove them back with baseball bats where they belonged. Then they called off the strike." [21]

This experience hardened the determination of Curran and the Communists and was the basis of their alliance. By October they were ready to try again and called a new shipping strike. This time crews poured off the ships, and when Dave Grange of the ISU tried to talk the men back onto the ships at a mass meeting at Cooper Union, he was hooted and whistled down. Then Curran called for a strike vote. He was seconded by Hedley Stone, a Communist and future treasurer of the National Maritime Union, and supported by the 1,500 seamen present.

The strike lasted ninety-nine days and cost twenty-seven lives, but it was won. And the new union, which joined the CIO at its first convention, was established. Aside from Curran, almost every leader of the National Maritime Union, from its formation in 1937 to the time of Curran's break with the left after World War II, was a party member. In the first six or seven years hundreds of rank and file party members made up the backbone of the union. But wartime cooperation with the shipowners and opposition to rank and file militancy lost the party many of its followers, and many more were lost to German submarines on the Murmansk run during the war (a disproportionately high number of Communists signed for this run). By the end of the war, when the NMU had 90,000 members, only 500 of them were Communists. However, for a careerist in the NMU, party membership was still a prerequisite. There were ports where the waterfront section of the party included every local official of the NMU but no rank and file seamen. [22]

The extent and meaning of Communist influence in the unions, especially in the CIO, are complicated questions. There is no doubt that Communists were important in organizing the CIO or that they had considerable influence and held many positions of authority in the various international unions and in the national office of the CIO. Party

[21] *Ibid.,* p. 95.
[22] *Ibid.,* pp. 98–99; interview with Al Richmond, February 1974.

members played different kinds of roles in different unions. Most CIO unions hired Communists as organizers; in a few, Communists had substantial followings among the rank and file and contested for power within the union; in several unions, Communists virtually ran the show. Party members had the greatest influence in unions like the ILWU and the NMU, where they had early abandoned the TUUL dual union and joined, or formed, insurgent rank and file movements in the old, corrupt, and minimally active AFL unions. In the NMU and ILWU party members were always subordinate to Curran and Bridges, but they established a central role for themselves and maintained it until after the War. In other unions, especially the United Automobile Workers and the United Electrical Workers (UE), Communists were not so central. Instead, they were one of several competing elements for control of the union. In the UAW, for example, Wyndham Mortimer was an early and very popular leader, but from the beginning he and his comrades were in competition with several other groups, some Socialist, some, like the followers of Homer Martin, the UAW's first elected president, politically conservative. Similarly, UE was formed as a coalition of some AFL federal radio locals, led by James B. Carey, and an electrical local at the General Electric home plant in Schenectady, led by Julius Emspak. Soon after UE was formed (March 1936), it was joined by several machinery locals that had belonged to the TUUL Steel and Metal Workers Industrial Union, led by James J. Matles. Both Emspak and Matles were Communists, and although Carey became president of UE, Matles and Emspak came to run the union.

In contrast, Communists had little power and small influence in the UMW and the Amalgamated Clothing Workers or other unions like them that had been AFL affiliates before the CIO was organized. If the Communists played any role in these unions it was as hired organizers or as rank and file militants in various locals. Similarly, in the Steel Workers Organizing Committee (SWOC) and later in the United Steelworkers of America, Communists served only as hired hands. They had muffed the opportunity to establish rank and file groups within the old Amalgamated Iron Workers union, and the CIO Steelworkers union was rigidly controlled from the top down by Philip Murray, a vice president of the UMW, who was appointed chairman of the SWOC by John L. Lewis.

In the formative stages of the CIO the Communists were a force for democracy because they functioned primarily as organizers of rank and file opposition caucuses in bureaucratic and ineffective unions. In the Third Period the Communists saw established trade union leaders as corrupt betrayers of working-class interests, and their agitation for industrial unions in the mass production industries expressed the needs and desires of most workers. Furthermore, Communists consistently fought for the rights of oppressed national groups in the workplace, especially for the equality of black workers within the unions. Thus, Communists generally represented the interests of the rank and file in the early 1930s and relied on workers in the shops for support and as their source of strength within the newly forming CIO unions.

A considerable difference existed between unions in which Communists were an important force and those with no organizational Communist presence. This was made clear at the founding convention of the United Steelworkers, for example, when Philip Murray announced in his keynote address that he would "fight any attempt to have little backroom caucuses while this convention is going on." Murray warned that if "any of the boys" were "thinking right now of midnight sessions in strange places in the city of Cleveland," they should "just begin to forget about it right now." And, of course, if midnight sessions were being planned, it was because daylight sessions would have been smashed by Murray's thugs.[23] Unlike the unions in the automobile industry, or on the docks, the Steelworkers were organized from the beginning from the top down. The Steel Workers Organizing Committee (SWOC) was set up by Lewis, who put up $500,000 of the Mine Workers' money and installed UMW vice president Philip Murray as chairman. Set up formally as a committee, the SWOC was actually dominated by Murray as thoroughly as the UMW was controlled by Lewis. As Len De Caux has written, "from the top down, SWOC was as totalitarian as any big business." That did not mean, however, that Communists did not work as SWOC organizers. Foster wrote that sixty of the initial organizers hired by SWOC were party members. But while the party organizers worked hard, they were carefully watched and

---

[23] See Art Preis, *Labor's Giant Step* (New York, 1964), p. 92; Len De Caux, *Labor Radical* (Boston, 1970), pp. 275–283.

mercilessly eliminated if they began to develop personal followings or if they failed to follow Murray's line.

But if unions without Communists were the least democratic, the converse was not always true. Many of the unions that Communists controlled retained democratic forms—monthly membership meetings, yearly conventions and elections of local and international officers, and elected shop stewards. This was particularly true of the UE, where a relatively high degree of membership participation was maintained and encouraged, especially by James Matles. Even so, the highest degree of participation and democratic control was in those unions where no one faction held unchallenged power. This was most true of the UAW, which, until Walter Reuther gained the presidency in 1946, was a cauldron of competing factions, none of which could eliminate the others and all of which vied for support of the rank and file. Most notably in the UAW, but also in a few other unions, the Communists were the most consistent upholders of democracy because they were usually the group least likely to be given support by Lewis, Sidney Hillman, or other CIO officials. Their strength depended more than anyone else's—except the relatively small Trotskyist splinters—on their support from the ranks. In unions tightly controlled by the party, democratic forms—regular membership meetings and elections—usually continued, but the democratic content often did not. This was clear in the NMU where becoming a union official was related to—if not absolutely dependent upon—one's attitude toward the party.

In addition, in the Popular Front Period (after 1935), party policy was to make alliances with liberals and with the trade union officials, and this often led to manipulation of the party's own members and their followers or supporters in the unions. This alliance, called the "Left-Center Bloc" in party jargon, was a working arrangement between the Communists and the CIO national leadership—Lewis, Hillman, and Murray—under which the party subordinated a socialist politics in return for a degree of toleration by the union leaders. In order to retain this alliance at the top the party was willing to ignore not only the desires of the workers but also the desires of its own militants and leaders within the various unions.

The most striking example of this occurred at the 1939 convention of the UAW. The convention's main purpose was to elect a new leadership in the wake of the expulsion of Homer Martin. The progressive caucus, led by Wyndham Mortimer and George Addes, had about 85 percent of the delegates. As Mortimer remembers it, the progressive caucus was undecided about whom to nominate, but it was a toss-up between Addes and himself. Mortimer was known as a far leftist (although he was not openly a Communist) and Addes, although a devout Catholic, was part of the left wing in the union. Sidney Hillman and Philip Murray both attended the convention. Their purpose was to push R. J. Thomas for president. The majority of delegates were clearly opposed to Thomas, a vice president who had been put in office by Martin and who had supported Martin until his expulsion. Hillman and Murray, of course, wanted to restrict the left and supported Thomas as a man they could control and use in their own power struggles within the CIO. The Communists, for their part, were committed to maintaining the Left-Center Bloc, which meant an alliance at the top with Hillman and Murray.

Although Murray and Hillman were open enemies of the left at this UAW convention—Murray made a speech attacking Mortimer and Addes—the party leadership was more concerned with retaining its alliance at the top than it was with developing solid political support among the rank and file. The Left-Center Bloc was put forward as necessary to the successful organization of the CIO, which in part it was. But if the CIO were to remain open to the left, rank and file participation and radicalization were also important. The party, however, subordinated its commitment to the workers and the building of a mass movement of the left to its relationship with the CIO bureaucracy. This was made clear when party leaders, including Earl Browder, came to the convention, buttonholed left-wing delegates, and pressured them into going along with Murray in support of R. J. Thomas. Mortimer resisted this pressure, but the combination of Murray's open attacks on the left and the party's pressure on its supporters was too great. Thomas was elected with the votes of the left. And the left began its decline in the UAW.[24]

But the problem of Communist policy was not simply the tactics of the Popular Front. Communist theory about the revolution and how it might be made was the underlying weakness, and this was not peculiar

---

[24] Mortimer, *op. cit.*, pp. 162–165; Richmond, *op. cit.*, pp. 241–243.

to the Popular Front but was a holdover from the Third Period. As long as the party was more concerned with its trade unionism, with the building of unions, than it was with building socialist consciousness among the workers, their espoused principles of democracy and equality could be sacrificed to the perpetuation of alliances at the top. Thus, during the Popular Front Period, Communists often made compromises that "betrayed" rank and file interests. They often acted undemocratically, and they even attacked struggles for the rights of blacks, as in the party's condemnation of A. Phillip Randolph's march on Washington (which forced Roosevelt to establish the Fair Employment Practices Commission during World War II). Nevertheless, generally the Communists stood for democracy and militancy in the unions, just as they were generally the most consistent defenders of the blacks and of their acceptance in the unions. Indeed, Communist militance and espousal of democratic rights in all spheres of public life were its main strong points during the Popular Front Period. This extended to foreign affairs, too. The heavy preponderance of Communists in the Abraham Lincoln Brigade—a group that went to Spain to help defend the Spanish Republic against Franco and his Nazi and fascist allies—and Communist opposition to Hitler only underlined this.

Of course, there was another strong point in the 1930s: the party's close ties to the Soviet Union. This had been of vital importance to the Communists' appeal among Socialists in the 1920s. In the 1930s the appeal broadened. While the American economy stagnated and millions of people desperately sought work, the Russians were in the midst of their five-year plans, had full employment, and were making rapid strides toward industrialization. It was difficult indeed in the 1930s to think of oneself as a revolutionary without identifying with the living embodiment of socialism triumphant. And, of course, the Communist Party had the franchise. Thus the party had the best of both worlds. It identified with the Bolsheviks and Revolution at the same time that it participated in democratic reforms and defended the highly popular Roosevelt Administration (although maintaining a mildly critical stance).

But this happy combination of assets was only temporary. It masked the party's fundamental flaw, which had been partially apparent in the 1920s and which would become fully apparent later on. In the 1920s, when the euphoria of the Russian Revolution was still fresh, and when the nature of advanced corporate capitalism was only beginning to become clear, the party's socialist credentials remained valid, if not perfect. This was especially so in the light of the developing anti-Sovietism in the Socialist Party, along with the latter's general paralysis. But if the Communist Party was credible as socialist in these years, the nature of its socialism—a simple parroting of the Soviet experience—prevented it from winning a substantial following. This had been part of the problem with the TUUL and it was generally so. "For a Soviet America," the party slogan of the pre-Popular Front years, was not, and could not be, an attractive vision for American workers, since it was based on emulating a society that was trying desperately to catch up with the industrialized West, particularly the United States, and under extremely harsh conditions. Thus, in the Third Period, the party was socialist but not popular. Then, during the Popular Front days the socialism disappeared but party activity was genuinely popular. By the 1960s it had neither popularity nor credibility as a socialist party.

Of course, party members had a private vision of socialism: the old one of a Soviet America. And in order to sustain themselves in their activity they had to have a theory of the revolutionary process that would make an apparently liberal politics credible as inherently revolutionary. Their private vision also provided the theory: a Soviet America would be achieved by the same process that enabled the Russian Socialists to seize power. Demands for bourgeois reform would create a pressure the capitalists could not satisfy, and a crisis would be precipitated. This understanding was historically determinist in the same sense that Eduard Bernstein's theory had been. It was based on the belief, officially expressed by the party at its ninth convention in 1936, that "a strong and consistent fight for democratic rights under conditions of decaying capitalism must ultimately lead the American people to the choice of a socialist path." Browder put it even more mechanistically: "History," he said, "marches toward socialism," and later: "Everything that organizes and activates the working class and its allies is progress toward socialism." [25] But, as subsequent experience has taught the left, and as some contemporary critics insisted, only a movement for socialism can march toward socialism. And if liberals organize and activate the working class it is to pursue their own ends.

[25] Browder, *op. cit.*, pp. 113, 263, 148.

This mode of thought led ultimately in the wrong direction. It made the Communists an unwitting but useful ally of liberal politicians and corporation leaders in adjusting the social system to the changed needs of the corporations. The Depression of the 1930s was unique not so much in its magnitude—although in 1933 one out of every three workers was unemployed (more than 15 million in all)—as in its duration. The Great Depression started in 1929 and did not end until 1940. And if it had not been for the massive arms production of World War II, it would not have ended then. By the 1930s, the rate of productivity in agriculture and in the mass production industries had increased to the point where fewer workers could produce an ever larger amount of goods. In this situation the "normal" business cycle no longer worked. The crisis itself could not sufficiently cheapen the cost of labor and capital nor could it create enough new demand to stimulate recovery. It now became necessary, for the first time, for the government to intervene on a massive scale to encourage and make possible mass consumption of consumer goods, especially consumer durables. Highway building programs, rural electrification, encouragement of suburbanization, the expansion of higher education, all had to be carried out or subsidized by the government. Ultimately even this was not enough and a permanent massive arms program became necessary.

In the 1930s the Roosevelt Administration was still only groping toward many of these policies, which in their initial stages were naturally popular. In a speech perfectly reflecting the ideology of this new liberalism, President Roosevelt declared that "in our generation a new idea has come to dominate thought about government—the idea that the resources of the nation can be made to produce a far higher standard of living for the masses if only government is intelligent and energetic in giving the right direction to economic life." This attempt by a capitalist government to regulate and stimulate the economy would have been branded fascist during the Third Period. In 1937 Browder welcomed Roosevelt's speech and announced that Communists "agree with its central thoughts and calmly and quietly tell the President that he has nothing to fear from us, but, on the contrary, will receive our help, as long as he really tries to carry out his declared program." [26] Neither response was able to comprehend the positive aspects of Roosevelt's

---

[26] Both quotations from Browder, *ibid.*, pp. 237, 240.

program while at the same time recognizing and explaining both the limitations of New Deal state capitalism and the ways in which it would create new needs and problems for the working class. The New Deal was neither proto-fascist nor proto-socialist. The goal of businessmen and politicians in the New Deal was, however, to get people back to work, to raise the standard of living, to provide people with a minimum level of security (but not enough so that they would not be forced to work at degrading and tedious jobs), and most of all to reduce class conflict by presenting themselves as champions of the ''common man.'' Unchallenged in their underlying purpose they could only emerge on top.

The tragedy of the Communist Party is clearest in the unions and in their own understanding of the meaning of their trade union work. Under capitalism, unions have at best a dual character. From the socialist point of view they are the primary form of the organization of workers as workers; they are the workers' most ''natural'' form of association and common ground of struggle. Because of this, any serious socialist party must relate to and be involved in union activity. Before the emergence of the new left all socialists understood this and the Communist Party was no exception. In the Third Period, however, the party isolated itself from the AFL, which despite all its corruption and weakness still represented the great mass of organized workers. This isolation was overcome, as we have seen, as the Third Period was abandoned and Communists entered first the old AFL unions and then helped organize the CIO. But precisely because unions are the natural organization of workers as workers, they will not develop class consciousness unless socialists actively intervene. As far as the corporate capitalists are concerned, unions are acceptable and even valuable to the degree that they stabilize the work force, help discipline the workers, and limit themselves to bargaining over wages and working conditions.

From the capitalist point of view unions can be accepted as a permanent institution only if they accept the framework of corporate capitalism and operate as a pressure group within it. In themselves, that is without the conscious intervention of liberal (capitalist) or socialist (working class) politics, the unions have no ''natural'' direction. But unions have never existed without this intervention from one side or both. In the early days of unionism, under competitive capitalism, most unions had a predominantly socialist consciousness, which is one of the reasons they were so fiercely resisted by employers. With the development of modern liberalism before World War I, the unions became an open battleground between socialists and liberal corporatists—working most notably in the National Civic Federation but also through other organizations and through Republican and Democratic party groups. In the 1920s (during the Third Period) the capitalist forces in the trade union movement had the AFL pretty much to themselves and the socialist forces worked through the TUUL in sectarian isolation. Finally, in the 1930s and beyond, the Communists became part of the mainstream of mass unionism but abandoned any struggle for an independent class politics. Thus it left liberal hegemony unchallenged within the AFL and the CIO.

Subordination to Liberalism

Except during its first two or three years (when it called for immediate insurrection), the Communist Party has never considered socialism an immediate issue. In the Third Period the party did publicize its version of socialism, but even then the Communists saw socialism as an issue for the indefinite future and centered its day-to-day practice on sectarian, militant trade union activity. After 1935, socialism receded even further as the party entered the mainstream and subordinated socialism to New Deal liberalism in its public activity. Both in the Third Period and during the Popular Front and after, Communists acted on the implicit assumption that through their activity around immediate demands, socialism would someday, somehow, become a public issue. They have never understood that socialism never does "become" a public issue: it must be *made* a public issue. Before he became a Communist, William Z. Foster put syndicalism in its crassest form when he wrote that the AFL was "making straight for the abolition of capitalism." In 1952, when he was chairman of the party, he no longer saw the unions as leaders of the revolutionary movement and was less optimistic about the timetable for socialism. But his underlying approach was similar: "The American working class," Foster wrote, was facing "developing crisis and destruction" and would "surely learn that the only way it can protect and improve its living standards is by taking the road that eventually leads to socialism." And, "The Communist Party holds the view that socialism in the United States, although inevitable in the future, is not now on the immediate political agenda."[27]

This was also the party position in 1938. True, the party platform mentioned socialism as "the highest form of democracy," which "lives and flourishes in one-sixth of the world, in the Soviet Union, where democracy triumphs." But in the same section of the platform it was made clear that "today the issue is not socialism or capitalism—the issue is democracy or fascism." The party insisted that the fight against the drive by finance capital toward a fascist United States was of paramount importance. As Browder later admitted (boasted is probably more accurate), the party moved "toward the broadest united front tactics of reformism for strictly limited aims. It relegated its revolutionary socialist goals to the ritual of chapel and Sundays on the pattern long followed by the Christian Church."[28]

This policy was mistaken on many levels. First, the "threat of fascism" has never been understood by the Communist Party in the United States or by most socialist sects. The Popular Front was instituted because of the threat that Germany posed to the Revolution in Russia, but it was accepted in the United States in the belief not only that "capitalism breeds fascism," but that under all circumstances large-scale corporate capitalism naturally moves toward fascism. The main tendency within the party was to believe that the ruling class prefers fascism to democratic rule. In the United States this led only to confusion and subordination to the liberals because the ruling class had little or no desire for fascism. Fascism is the abandonment of constitutional rule. It means the elimination of established formal democracy in favor of open dictatorship. Fascism requires public coercion and is an admission that capitalists can no longer rule with the consent of the population at large. No ruling class, at least no rational ruling class, will move toward open dictatorial rule if it can continue to disguise its rule thrugh a formal democracy. What would it gain? It is true that advanced capitalism raises the threat of fascism, but that is because it becomes harder and harder to

---

[27] First quotation from James Weinstein, *The Decline of Socialism in America, 1912–1925* (New York, 1967), p. 262; second and third quotation from Foster, *History CPUSA* (New York, 1952), pp. 549, 552–553.

[28] Earl Browder, "The American Communist Party in the Thirties," in Rita Simon, ed., *As We Saw the Thirties* (Urbana, Ill., 1967), p. 237.

maintain support for corporate policies and goals. But it is only at the point that formal democratic rule begins to break down, when the existing constitutional methods of rule no longer work, and then only if a socialist movement is threatening to take power, that a ruling class will give its primary support to fascist groups. This is what happened in Italy in the 1920s and in Germany in the early 1930s. But it is not what happened or was about to happen in the United States in the 1930s.

Indeed, the opposite was true: the most advanced elements among the corporate leadership supported Roosevelt and his New Deal policies, even in the face of fears among many big businessmen that Roosevelt was going too far in placating the American masses. Of course, socialism did not present itself as an issue in the 1930s. The issue was between the liberalism of the New Deal, put forward by corporate liberal politicians and businessmen, and the traditionalism (nineteenth-century liberalism) of the more conservative businessmen and politicians. This division was between different corporate interests, and even though workers overwhelmingly supported the New Deal, it did not represent a working-class alternative. Socialism did not emerge as an issue because the Communists never put forth a serious socialist position for which to argue as an alternative to the New Deal. They did not attempt to organize a popular party for socialism. Thus, despite the favorable position the Communists had in the trade union movement, they were unable to take advantage of the Great Depression in the way they anticipated. In the 1920s, they had believed that a depression would create a working-class socialist consciousness and an insurrection. But instead of taking power with the collapse of the economy, the Communist Party succeeded only in temporarily gaining control of many union offices. It became part of the bureaucracy.

This is not to say that the CIO was not political. From its inception it was intimately tied to and dependent upon politics and politicians—to the Democratic Party and Democrats. This was true on all levels of union activity. On top, John L. Lewis lobbied relentlessly to get Section 7a written into the National Recovery Act in 1933. Lewis's biographer, perhaps exaggerating a little, writes that Lewis "had staked everything" on Section 7a's inclusion in the NRA. And when the NRA was enacted with this section, Lewis hired dozens of organizers and threw the entire treasury of the UMW into an organizing campaign under the slogan "the President wants you to join the union." Thousands upon thousands responded and streamed back into the union they had recently abandoned with disgust. In two years UMW membership increased from 100,000 to more than 400,000.[29]

Lewis began arguing for Section 7a even before he decided to organize the Committee for Industrial Organization within the AFL. Section 7a was formulated as part of the proposed NRA at a meeting in the home of financier Bernard Baruch, who had been head of the War Industries Board during World War I and was an early adviser of Franklin Roosevelt. As Lewis remembered the meeting, several top industrialists, including the chairman of the board of Standard Oil, were present and agreed to the NRA with the guarantee of labor's right to organize.[30] This implied, since the meeting was held at Roosevelt's suggestion, a close relationship between Lewis (and the new unions in general) and the Roosevelt Administration. And that relationship remained close, so close that when Lewis, who was clearly the dominant personality in the CIO, split with Roosevelt in 1940, he was unable to take the CIO out of the Democratic Party's camp and was himself forced to resign from the CIO presidency.

The argument that union activity, or struggle in the workplace, would lead to socialist consciousness even in the absence of a public socialist movement contesting for state power neglects the activity of the liberal capitalists and of the union bureaucrats. In the 1930s, as always, both groups sought close alliances between the unions and the major political parties, especially the Democratic Party, which emerged in the 1930s as the friend of the "common man" in his battle against the "economic royalists." On a national level, this alliance was crucial to the relatively quick success of the CIO, particularly in several early key strikes.

The central importance of government mediation, and of the alliance with the Democrats, has been glossed over in most left accounts of strikes like the General Motors sit-down strike at Flint, Michigan, and the San Francisco general strike. But at Flint, Governor Frank Murphy's role was all important, and in San Francisco the National Long-

[29] Alinsky, *op. cit.*, p. 71.
[30] *Ibid.*, pp. 66–67.

shoremen's Board (created by Roosevelt in June 1934) was important in formulating the final terms of the settlement, especially the establishment of the union hiring hall. Of course, neither strike could have been won without the militant and united activity of the workers, both those who started the strikes and those who supported them. But in Flint a hostile governor could have called in the National Guard to enforce the court order enjoining the strikers that General Motors had secured. If he had done so, the bloody result would have been a defeat for the union. Most state governors probably would have done so, and Murphy himself almost did. It was only John L. Lewis's constant pressure on the governor that convinced him at the last minute not to issue an order to bring in the troops. When this happened, General Motors capitulated and the strike was won.[31]

In San Francisco the strike was much stronger, had wider working-class support, and involved several direct confrontations between the strikers and the police—especially after the battle of Rincon Hill on Bloody Thursday, July 5, 1934. These events led to the general strike, which began eleven days later and forced through a victory for the longshoremen. But even during the height of the confrontations, the National Longshoremen's Board held public hearings and provided a forum for Bridges to explain the strikers' side of events to the people of San Francisco. And when the strike was settled, the final terms were decided by the board, which arbitrated between the union and the employers.[32]

The top union bureaucrats were not the only ones who sought a measure of political power. Local workers and unionists also understood the importance of gaining some independent political strength in their cities. In western Pennsylvania, for example, "there were no labor 'friends' in local government" in the 1920s and early 1930s, wrote George Powers, a former rank and filer and organizer for the SWOC. In McKeesport and surrounding cities, "steel management ran both the Republican Party and the local government." But as the SWOC became active in the mills in 1936 and 1937, the new lodges "could not remain indifferent to the problem of political powerlessness." These new locals

[31] *Ibid.*, pp. 97–146, especially p. 145.
[32] Larrowe, *op. cit.*, pp. 66–92.

were the largest organizations in their various communities and had "young and vigorous leadership." In McKeesport, the new local called a meeting of all local labor unions, fraternal, civic, and political organizations. In addition to the steel locals, representatives came from the miners' union, the Central Labor Union, the bartenders, printers, the unemployed, the Croation Fraternal Lodge, the Polish National Alliance, the Greek and Italian clubs, and the local Democratic Party, officially represented by its chairwoman, Mrs. Gertrude O'Shea. The slates chosen were coalitions of unionists and Democrats (each group choosing candidates of its own and retaining independence of action). In Duquesne, for example, the candidate was Elmer J. Malloy, president of the SWOC lodge, and in Clairton, John Mullen, president of his lodge, headed the ticket. This new movement was a big success in 1937. In the November elections seventeen steel communities voted in "labor-liberal coalitions," thereby ending decades of tight control by the steel corporations.[33]

The intimate relationship between the CIO and the Democrats was only the most recent example of the constant and close relationship of trade unionism to politics. Gompers and the AFL had become increasingly dependent on negotiations both with the state and with informal groups of corporation leaders, although as the AFL became less active in organizing the unorganized they commanded less attention both from politicians and businessmen. Republican and Democratic businessmen and politicians had been more attentive to Gompers and other AFL leaders when the Federation had still shown signs of aggressive organizing—and when the Socialist Party was actively competing for the votes and support of union members. Before and during World War I, the Socialists had won the support of substantial minorities in many AFL unions and of majorities in some (the Machinists, Mine, Mill, and Smelter Workers, Amalgamated Clothing Workers, Brewery Workers, and others). They did so on the basis of the party's general politics and in conjunction with electoral activity not only on a national level but especially in cities and towns where industrial workers were a majority. Indeed, in the western Pennsylvania region that saw the creation of

---

[33] See George Powers, *Cradle of Steel Unionism: Monongahela Valley, Pa.* (East Chicago, Ind., 1972), Ch. 10. This is a privately printed history of the early steel union days by a local participant and leader.

labor-Democratic alliances in the 1930s, the Socialists had elected some mayors and several city councilmen before and during World War I.[34] In the 1930s, as Powers points out, labor—at least on the local level— did not want to "remain the passive tail to the Democratic machine." As Powers saw it, "Labor emerged the champion of the principles of democaracy" in 1937.[35] But, in fact, especially since the top CIO leadership was so intimately committed to Roosevelt, local labor was willy-nilly pulled into the Democratic Party.

This happened, at least in part, because the Communists believed that socialism was not on the agenda in the 1930s and because they had no independent socialist politics except their private commitment to the Bolsheviks. This commitment was not to Marxism or Leninism, although lip service was paid to both, but to the specific Russian understanding of internal and international problems. In this period, just as much as in the Third Period, the Communist Party exactly met Lenin's definition of economism. They were convinced that it was possible "to develop the class political consciousness of the workers *from within,* so to speak, from their economic struggle"—by "making this struggle the exclusive (or, at least, the main) starting point." But, as Lenin insisted, the only sphere from which the workers could develop class consciousness is "the sphere of relations *of all* classes and strata to the state and the government, the sphere of the interrelations between *all* classes." [36]

For their own private purposes, however, to convince the party members and win recruits, the party had to have some rationale that would put forward the prospect of moving toward an openly socialist politics—no matter how slowly. Thus, in 1936, when Lewis and Hillman organized Labor's Non-Partisan League on a national scale and the American Labor Party in New York, the party hailed this as a step toward an independent labor party, for which the Communists energetically agitated.[37] In fact, the League and the American Labor Party were organized and widely understood outside the left simply as a means to win labor votes for Roosevelt—"to allow Socialists and others on the

---

[34] Socialists elected mayors in New Castle, Pitcairn, McKeesport (Controller), and Martin's Ferry, Ohio, in these years.

[35] Powers, *op. cit.,* p. 142.

[36] V. I. Lenin, *What Is to Be Done?* (Moscow, 1969), pp. 78–79.

[37] Foster, *op. cit.,* pp. 332–333.

left to vote for Democratic candidates on a non-Democratic slate,'' as Irving Bernstein accurately points out.[38] The effect of the American Labor Party in New York was to eliminate the remaining effectiveness of the Socialists as an electoral party (Norman Thomas had received 885,000 votes in 1932, and the Socialists were strong in New York City) and to transfer rank and file Socialist voters into the Democratic Party. To underline this meaning, both David Dubinsky of the International Ladies Garment Workers Union and Emil Rieve of the Hosiery Workers publicly resigned from the Socialist Party and announced their support of Roosevelt.

Of course, given their initial weakness and isolation in the early 1930s, the Communists could not have prevented Lewis and other CIO leaders from allying with Roosevelt and the New Deal. But that is not the point. It was entirely possible in the '30s, especially for a party with as strong a base in the unions as the Communists had, to contest as socialists in the electoral arena and to build a popular socialist movement among millions of workers and unemployed. Certainly in hundreds of industrial cities and towns labor-socialist alliances could have been attempted in place of the labor-Democratic coalitions that were established. The Communists rejected this path for many reasons. The most obvious was their subservience to the Russians and to current Russian policy, which dictated a common front with the liberals against (in the United States) a nonexistent fascist threat. This policy was consistent with the basically syndicalist (economist) understanding of the revolutionary process that has pervaded the entire socialist movement in the United States, starting with the left wing of the old Socialist Party before World War I. And, of course, these factors were strengthened by the mass movement into the CIO, the realization of the longtime dream of Socialists to organize workers in the mass production industries along industrial lines.

Communists argued then, and in retrospect still assert, that this was the only path that could have been followed, that it was ''politic'' or ''realistic.'' But in the end, even in the narrow organizational sense, the Popular Front was self-defeating. Because the Communists' public politics was indistinguishable from that of the left-wing liberals, the

[38] Bernstein, *op. cit.,* p. 449.

basis of their power within the unions rested on two things: 1) their organizational strength, experience, and commitment and 2) their working relations with the top leadership of the CIO. The value of the Communists and the basis of their alliance with Lewis, Hillman, Murray, etc., was their organizing ability and a substantial measure of control in several new unions. Increasingly, the Communists sacrificed rank and file militancy and political support among the rank and file for close working relations with the top leaders. But as the CIO became established, as it accomplished its basic organizing goals, developed a bureaucratic structure of its own, and secured legal recognition and institutionalized working relations—through the National Labor Relations Board—with the government and the employers, the Communists became less and less needed by CIO leaders and their potential liabilities increased. (After all, the party professed to be socialist and always presented the possibility of developing a socialist politics.) Thus, as the party became less and less necessary to the CIO leadership, its position of strength in the CIO in general became more and more dependent on its relations with the top leaders. The end was inevitable. Without an independent political base in the unions, without a socialist movement among the workers, the party's position was more and more at the sufferance of the CIO leaders. These men—Murray, Hillman, Reuther—were both anti-socialist and anti-Communist and only awaited an opportunity to dump the left. When that opportunity came, the Communists' own closest allies—Joe Curran in the NMU and Michael Quill in the Transport Workers Union—practical trade unionists that they were, abandoned the party too. When the cold war started, the Communists' only identifiable political difference with the other left liberals was their support of the Soviet Union and their opposition to the alliance between the CIO leadership and the State Department. But, especially given their longtime relationship and subordination to the Soviet Union, this issue had to be a losing one and in fact became the opportunity to purge the Communists from the left-wing unions. In 1949 they were purged.

In the Third Period the Communists had sacrificed popularity for an ahistorical socialism. During the Popular Front they sacrificed even this socialism for a transitory popularity. They did so in both instances in the name of Lenin and Leninism, but both times they violated Lenin's basic tenets. Lenin's politics were a giant step forward in the development of Marxist politics, but literally translated to the United States, "Bolshevism" was a step backward from parliamentary socialism to militant syndicalism (interest-group politics)—a politics that led directly into co-optation by the corporate liberals of the New Deal. The worldwide effect of the Russian Revolution was to advance revolutionary movements in the colonies and semi-colonies and to retard it in the industrialized West. In countries like China, and later in Vietnam and Cuba, where the capitalist class had not yet established its hegemony, socialist revolutionaries were able to turn bourgeois goals for national independence and formal democratic rights to their advantage. In the pre-capitalist nations and semi-colonies, where during the 1920s the International stressed the possibility of socialist revolution, the similarities to the Russian situation worked largely to the advantage of the revolutionaries. But in the developed capitalist nations a similar strategy strengthened the hand of the capitalist ruling classes.

4/

BLACKS AND THE LEFT

The International's early orientation toward revolutionary activity in the colonies and semi-colonies had one major positive effect in the United States. It focused attention on the "Negro Question" and led to the development of a theory of black oppression that in many respects marked a major advance over earlier socialist and radical parties. At the heart of the Communist position was the understanding that the Negro Question was a national question, and that the Negro population in the black belt of the South constituted a nation within a nation. This, in turn, implied a dual revolutionary process, with the blacks' struggle for national liberation taking place side by side with the socialist revolution, in contrast to the traditional view of the fight against racism and discrimination against Negroes as entirely subsumed under the need for working-class unity and the fight for socialism. As a result of this understanding, the party's activity among blacks and for Negro rights was vastly increased, and within the party there were continuing efforts to eradicate white chauvinist attitudes among party members and to advance blacks into party leadership.

In its early years, although Communists opposed racism and made some attempts to recruit blacks, the party's record was not substantially better than the Socialists' had been. As early as 1903, Debs insisted that "as a socialist party we receive the Negro and all other races upon absolutely equal terms." And the party itself invited "the Negro to membership and fellowship with us in the world movement for economic emancipation by which equal liberty and opportunity shall be secured to every man and fraternity become the order of the world." [1] Of course, the Socialist Party's actual record was spotty. In a period of intense and intensifying racism, Socialists were subject to the prevailing social pressures, and not all of them lived up to the party's principles. But as the party grew and consolidated its ideas, Socialists were more consistent in their anti-racism. By 1913 most of the southern state parties had black members, although in a few states they were in separate locals. Later, when large numbers of blacks moved north during the war, the party developed a substantial Negro membership in New York centered around A. Phillip Randolph and Chandler Owen's magazine, *The Messenger*. [2]

In contrast, and despite prodding from Lenin and other leaders of the International, the Communist Party had only two dozen black members as late as 1927.[3] But there had been a running debate on the Negro Question in Moscow, starting at the Second Congress of the Comintern in 1920. This discussion reached a conclusion in late 1928 at the Sixth Congress, with the adoption of the position that Negroes constituted a nation in the black belt of the southern United States. As the *Daily Worker* then explained, this meant that "while continuing and intensifying the struggle under the slogan of full social and political equality for Negroes," the party "must come out openly and unreservedly for the right of Negroes to national self-determination in the southern states where Negroes form a majority of the population." [4]

The 1928 "Thesis" of the International was part of its program for building revolutionary movements in the "Colonies and Semi-

---

[1] Arthur Schlesinger, Jr., ed., *Eugene V. Debs, Writings and Speeches* (New York, 1948), pp. 65, 68.

[2] Socialists ran several black candidates for the State Legislature in New York, and Randolph was the party's candidate for State Comptroller in 1920. He received 200,000 votes. See James Weinstein, *The Decline of Socialism in America, 1912–1925* (New York, 1968), pp. 63–74.

[3] Theodore G. Vincent, *Black Power and the Garvey Movement* (Berkeley, 1971), p. 82.

[4] Theodore Draper, *American Communism and Soviet Russia* (New York, 1957), pp. 349–351.

Colonies'' and profoundly changed the attitude of the American party. During previous years the party had made sporadic attempts to attract blacks, most notably when Cyril Briggs and several other leaders of the African Blood Brotherhood had joined in late 1921 and again in 1924 when the Communists unsuccessfully tried to establish fraternal relations with Marcus Garvey's Universal Negro Improvement Association. But, in fact, Briggs and other black nationalists within the party found that only in Russia were they able to get much attention. The real debates on the Negro Question went on there for seven years before they had substantial effect in the United States.[5] After the International's decision in 1928 the American party debated its meaning for more than a year. Then in late 1930 a final resolution of the International led to intensive activity around the new program.

Although the call for an independent black republic in the South attracted little support, the party's subsequent concentration on the Negro Question quickly gained it considerable following among blacks. In the North, the party concentrated on legal defense, unemployment, and discrimination in hiring and in the unions. The Scottsboro case, a frame-up on rape charges of nine young blacks in Alabama in 1931, was the most publicized of the Communist defense activities during the Third Period. Their activity won them the hostility and distrust of all the liberals who worked on the case. But it also won them a measure of respect and support among blacks. This activity, combined with organizing unemployed councils and fighting for Negro rights through the TUUL unions, won blacks to the party in the early 1930s. In one party district that included Illinois, Indiana, and parts of Wisconsin, Iowa, and Missouri, the party increased its membership among blacks from 50 to 700 between 1930 and 1932.[6]

By the late 1930s there were 8,000 to 10,000 black Communists, more than 10 percent of the party membership, most of them in Harlem and Chicago. These gains resulted from a combination of militant activity in behalf of civil rights, mostly in the North, and the party's support for self-determination in the South (and their intention to fight for it once a party base could be established there), which disarmed black na-

---

[5] *Ibid.*, Ch. 15.
[6] John Williamson, *Dangerous Scot* (New York, 1969), p. 91.

tionalists.[7] As a result of its activity during the 1930s, the party succeeded for the first time in building a substantially interracial movement, with itself at the center.

Yet, largely because of the theory on which the party acted, the results were not all positive and were short-lived. The party's racial politics was based on the idea of independence for an agrarian nation of blacks. But the path of black development was already going in another direction as can be seen clearly in retrospect. Modernization of agriculture and the rapid growth of cities, North and South, combined to push blacks off the land and into urban industrial or service jobs. Rather than remaining peasants (which is how Communists understood them), blacks steadily entered the working class. The proletarianization of blacks had been accelerated by World War I and continued with the integration of the corporate capitalist economy in the United States. The first of the major black nationalist movements, Marcus Garvey's Universal Negro Improvement Association, was a post-World War I, primarily northern and urban movement that stood for the independence of African and West Indian colonies and took pride in the African heritage and blackness of Negroes. The Garvey movement did not understand itself as proletarian. In fact, its best-known project was an all-black shipping line, the Black Star Line. But the Garvey movement attracted hundreds of thousands of blacks and was clearly both northern and urban. This character of 1920s black nationalism was ignored by the Communists because their position on American blacks did not derive from an analysis of the United States but by analogy with Asian and African nations, which were, indeed, pre-capitalist, predominantly peasant societies.

As the party understood things, the revolutionary content of its program consisted of the demand for national self-determination in the South, while its day-to-day politics consisted of struggles for civil rights. The main thrust of party activity was for legal rights and integration, particularly within the unions. Since the party understood the revolutionary aspect of its policy on the Negro question as one of national independence—as a "bourgeois" demand of non-proletarians (peasants)—and since, in fact, the most pressing demands of blacks were for

---

[7] Vincent, *op. cit.*, pp. 233 ff.

elementary democratic rights, it is no surprise that socialism was considered even less important as a public issue for blacks than for whites. Even though the party did not put forward the need for socialism in its public activity, white party members were often educated in the Marxist classics and Communist theory. But the party did not educate its black members—except those chosen for leadership—in the same way. As a result, as George Blake Charney, the party's second in command in Harlem from 1937 to 1942 (and a white), writes of this period: "For most [blacks], the relationship of the freedom struggle to socialism was nebulous, even irrelevant." Indeed, he concluded, "We never quite knew to what degree, if any, the idea of socialism penetrated the minds of party members" in Harlem.[8]

The party's understanding of Negro liberation as an agrarian question reinforced its conception of itself as the vanguard party and strengthened its opposition to autonomous black revolutionary movements. This was so because it understood itself as the party of the working class, which had the duty of leading other classes to socialist politics. Since blacks were seen as peasants, by and large, their own movements could only have a bourgeois nationalist consciousness. The idea of an independent black socialist movement was incomprehensible in this period. Black nationalist movements were understood as anti-working class. Of course, at the same time, the party recognized the need for blacks to participate in all-white working-class organizations and also for them to have their "own national organizations." But these organizations were explicitly non-revolutionary—the NAACP, the Negro National Labor Council (a Communist Party front), fraternal organizations, and business institutions.[9] Genuinely autonomous (all black) nationalist movements were militantly opposed by the party both before and after it abandoned the idea of a Negro nation in the South in

---

[8] George Blake Charney, *A Long Journey* (Chicago, 1968), p. 105. Note the similarity in Charney's way of understanding the lack of socialist consciousness among black party members and the general Communist understanding of the reasons that "socialism was not an issue." In both cases the implicit assumption is that socialism will become an issue on its own, that the party must follow the spontaneous political development of its constituencies rather than provide political leadership and initiative.

[9] See William Z. Foster, *The Negro People in American History* (New York, 1954), p. 560.

the late 1950s. Thereafter, the party returned to a liberal integrationist line and opposed the new revolutionary nationalist movements, best represented by Malcolm X, until the late 1960s when Communists briefly supported the Black Panther Party.

5/

THE COMMUNIST PARTY DURING WORLD WAR II

/ Militance Goes to War

By the end of the 1930s Communists could hardly be distinguished from militant New Dealers except in their unswerving loyalty to the Soviet Union and its immediate national interests—and in their almost purely private commitment to socialist revolution. The party's relationship to the Russians did place it in opposition to Roosevelt from the signing of the Nazi-Soviet pact and the invasion of Poland in 1939 until the invasion of the Soviet Union by Germany in June 1941. But this opposition was strictly concerned with foreign policy. Once the Russians were fighting the Germans and the United States entered the war, the Communists became militant patriots and win-the-war advocates. Indeed, they became so patriotic that they opposed both trade union and civil rights militancy that appeared in any way to "disrupt" the war effort—especially if that militancy was led by political enemies like the Trotskyist Socialist Workers Party or the Socialist A. Phillip Randolph.

One of the more striking examples of the Communists' subservience to the immediate interests of the Soviet Union as they understood it was the party's condemnation of the March on Washington Movement led by Randolph. The March on Washington Movement included the NAACP, the National Urban League, and Randolph's Brotherhood of

Sleeping Car Porters (AFL). Its program called for equal employment opportunities for blacks in defense industries and better treatment in the armed services (which were almost entirely segregated), but the movement was not anti-war. The movement did plan a massive march on Washington in support of its program and the march was averted only when Roosevelt issued an executive order (No. 8802) setting up the Fair Employment Practices Commission. In short, the march helped to force Roosevelt to give at least token recognition of Negro rights during the war. This activity was condemned by the party as "sabotaging the war effort" and of sowing "confusion and dangerous moods in the rank and file of the Negro people and utilizing their justified grievances as a weapon of opposition to the Administration's war program." [1]

Randolph was singled out by the party as a particular villain, as a "fascist helping defeatism," a saboteur, etc. [2] Ironically, Randolph had earlier gotten into conflict with the party, when, as president of the National Negro Congress, a Communist front organized in 1936, he had opposed their attempt to convert the Congress into an anti-war organization. This occurred in the time between the signing of the Nazi-Soviet pact and the invasion of the Soviet Union, during which the party insisted that "the Yanks are not coming" and attacked Roosevelt as a war monger. [3]

The party's abandonment of blacks in the interest of national unity during the war was matched by its abandonment of civil liberties for dissenters and union militants. This was particularly clear in regard to the first prosecution under the Smith Act of 1940. The Smith Act made it a crime to teach or advocate the overthrow of the United States government, or to conspire to do so, and also required the fingerprinting and registration of aliens in the United States. Although Communist Party leaders were to be the main victims of the Smith Act during the cold war, the first prosecution under the act took place in 1941, when

---

[1] Quoted in Irving Howe and Lewis Coser, *The American Communist Party* (Boston, 1957), p. 415.

[2] *Daily Worker,* December 18, 1944, quoted in *ibid.*

[3] For example, in an Almanac Singers' song of those years, Roosevelt was parodied as follows: "Oh, I hate war and so does Eleanor, but we won't be safe 'til everybody's dead." On Randolph and the National Negro Congress, see Wilson Record, *Race and Radicalism* (Ithaca, 1964), p. 115.

twenty-nine leaders of Teamsters Local 544 in Minneapolis—most of whom were members of the Socialist Workers Party—were indicted and tried. Local 544 had been under the control of Trotskyists since the early 1930s, when the Dunne brothers had led the Minneapolis general strike. In 1941 the local decided to quit the International Brotherhood of Teamsters and join the CIO. At this point Daniel Tobin, president of the Teamsters and chairman of the Democratic Party's National Labor Committee, called on Roosevelt for help. Claiming that the local quit the Teamsters because the union stood behind the government and that the local consisted of "enemies of the government," he condemned the CIO "raid" of his union as disruptive of the war effort. Roosevelt's response was to indict the leaders of Local 544 in a bald political payoff to Tobin.

The Communists, who had opposed passage of the Smith Act and deplored its use, nevertheless boasted that it had "always exposed, fought against and today joins the fight to exterminate the Troskyite Fifth Column from the life of our nation." [4] This attitude was possible because the Communists were all-out for the war, while the Trotskyists were not. But it also reflected their long-standing view of Trotsky's followers as akin to the Nazis.

Despite these regressions on the part of the Communists, the war was a great boon to their immediate fortunes. For now the Russians were the allies of the Americans and were being portrayed, even in the movies, as friendly, likable folks. The party's close ties to the Soviets now became another point in common with the New Deal and Roosevelt. To further this identification and to reduce the stigma of the party as a foreign agent (it was affiliated with the Third International until 1940, when the party formally dissolved its ties to conform to the Voorhis Act; the International as a whole dissolved in 1943), the party itself dissolved and became the Communist Political Association (CPA). This step made it easier for people to affiliate with the Communists and was successful from the point of view of membership and acceptability to other liberal organizations. When the war ended in Europe (May 1945), the Communist Political Association had about 70,000

---

[4] *Daily Worker*, August 16, 1941, quoted in Art Preis, *Labor's Giant Step* (New York, 1964), p. 141.

members, an all-time high. More than one-fifth of the CIO membership was in unions led by Communists or their allies, and the CPA could count on one-third of the vote on the executive board of the CIO. In addition, in New York City the Communists elected two members to the city council in 1945 (one black, Benjamin Davis, the other an Italian, Pete Caccione), and two of the American Labor Party councilmen worked closely with the CPA.[5] In general, and particularly in liberal and labor circles, the Communists were a force to be reckoned with and to be respected.

The Cold War Begins

From 1935 to 1945 the Communists had succeeded in becoming part of the Popular Front against fascism. They had done so by abandoning even their narrow attempts to make socialism a public issue and by submerging themselves first in building the CIO and then in all-out support of the wartime alliance with the Soviet Union. But by 1945 the CIO had been built, the war was over, and the United States was beginning to assume its postwar responsibilities as the center and primary defender of the world capitalist system. The Soviets, of course, were the main enemy. And the Communists, no longer the beneficiaries of the Popular Front against fascism, quickly became the chief victims of the new Popular Front against Communism.

The options open to the Communists by the end of the war were limited by their own history and by the sweep of events. Although it had failed to create a self-conscious movement for socialism, the party still had an apparently formidable trade union base and pro-Soviet policies to sustain it. Within the unions, however, most of the Communists or pro-Communists in leadership no longer needed the party cadre or party support to retain their power. The unions were built; contracts were in effect; labor relations were institutionalized. Once it became clear that association with the party was more of a liability than an asset, the party's alliances with the trade union bureaucracy were doomed. And once the liberals adopted the cold war as their basic strategy for post-World War II expansionism, their toleration of the Communists ended.

[5] See David Shannon, *The Decline of American Communism* (New York, 1953), Ch. 1.

The result was a rapid collapse of what on the surface appeared to be a solid political position.

Within the party this situation was at best dimly understood. In early 1944 Browder wrote that in his "considered judgment" the American people were "so ill-prepared subjectively for any deep-going change in the direction of socialism" that public discussion or agitation for socialism "would not unite the nation but would further divide it." That national unity under the leadership of corporate capital should be the goal of a "communist" party was not questioned at the time because, as Browder explained, to agitate for socialism would divide the liberals and the Communists and "help the anti-Teheran forces to come to power in the United States." "Teheran" meant postwar cooperation between the United States and the Soviet Union, and Browder's remarks simply reflected the priority given to the support of Soviet foreign policy by the party. "If the national unity of the war period is to be extended and even strengthened in the postwar period," Browder concluded, then "this requires from Marxists the reaffirmation of our wartime policy that we will not raise the issue of socialism in such a form and manner as to endanger or weaken national unity." [6]

Browder's policy statements were reflected in the changed attitude of even the most militant of the left-wing unions. Harry Bridges, for example, told his union that he envisioned a postwar world of cooperation between capitalists and labor, one in which the workers would not challenge their position as workers. Under the union's proposed postwar no-strike pledge, Bridges explained, employers would "be free to participate in the worldwide expansion of trade and economy that we visualize," while labor would "participate through security in their jobs, their fundamental conditions, and their unions." [7] The wartime no-strike policy of the party and its followers was to be extended indefinitely, in other words.

Within the party this line was virtually unchallenged. William Z. Foster was almost alone in opposing Browder's view of harmonious postwar relations between the United States and the Soviets, and he did

[6] Earl Browder, *Teheran and America* (New York, 1944), p. 19. This pamphlet is text of Browder's January 1944 national committee report.

[7] *Proceedings*, Sixth Biennial Convention at San Francisco, March 29–April 2, 1945, International Longshoremen's and Warehousemen's Union, pp. 44–45.

not press his differences once it became clear that he had no support among the party leadership. But Foster's views more nearly reflected world realities than did Browder's, and it was only a matter of time before the American party was given a signal by its European comrades that a change in line was needed. This was the famous Duclos letter, an article by Jacques Duclos in the French Communist magazine *Cahiers du Communisme*, which concluded that Browder was the "protagonist of a false concept of social evolution" in the United States.[8] Armed with this formidable backing, and with Duclos's implicit support, Foster now moved against Browder quickly and decisively. Foster's own position, which had remained private within high party circles, was now made public; Browder's position was repudiated by virtually all party leaders; and Browder himself was subjected to scathing criticism and denunciation by his closest former followers. The Communist Political Association was abandoned and the party formally reconstituted, and Browder, the preeminent leader and public figure in the American Communist movement for the previous decade, was summarily expelled.

At the time, and in later years, Foster and other Communist leaders presented Browder's repudiation and expulsion as a repudiation of "revisionism" and "social democratic" policies and as a return to "Leninism." [9] But, in fact, except for a new militant line on the Negro Question (including a revival of the idea of a Negro nation in the black belt), the reconstituted party under Foster was little different from the CPA under Browder in its basic understanding of the role of a socialist party. The major difference, of course, was in regard to the prospects for peaceful coexistence with the Soviets. But that question would have been answered the same way even if Browder had remained in control, since it was not only a theoretical question but one quickly answered by American policymakers at the end of the war. In other respects, the

[8] Quoted in Joseph Starobin, *American Communism in Crisis, 1943–1957* (Cambridge, Mass., 1972), pp. 78–79.

[9] See, for example, Foster's description of Browder and his policies in the *History of the Communist Party of the United States* (New York, 1952), Ch. 30. Foster writes that "in the present period of sharp domestic class struggle [1952], international war danger, and the Leninist position of the Communist Party, it seems almost incredible that the party could ever have made the fundamental error of accepting Browder's impossible Teheran scheme" (p. 427).

party remained basically the same—hardly any closer to Lenin than Browder had been.

Like Browder, Foster believed that socialism would "not be a political issue in the United States in the early postwar period." Foster did criticize Browder for "underestimating the democratic masses" and for overestimating "their acceptance of the bourgeois leadership of the two main parties." But his idea of how socialism would become an issue was based purely on "objective" factors and led to the same passivity and liberalism that Browder's view did. "Mass interest in socialism," Foster predicted, would be generated by the "world-shaking demonstration of power and success" of the Soviets, by their "miracles" of postwar reconstruction. This, and other countries following the Soviet lead, were expected to arouse the interest of Americans in socialism.[10] Foster's most effective argument, though clothed in rhetoric about Browder's "revisionism" and "American exceptionalism," rested on his correct anticipation of the cold war and on the need for the party militantly to oppose American postwar expansionism. In addition, Foster had a gut commitment to the class struggle as he understood it and an instinctive revulsion of Browder's vision of domestic class harmony.

Yet within the framework of opposition to the cold war and a return to militance within the unions and within the party around such questions as the struggle against white chauvinism and male supremacy, the party's policy was a continuation of the basic political principles embodied in the Popular Front. Even after 1945, the party supported a liberal capitalist program that subordinated socialism to the immediate interests of trade unionists and blacks in order to achieve unity with liberals who opposed the anti-Soviet policies of the government. The Popular Front had been an alliance of Communists with liberals in power.

[10] Quoted in Starobin, *op. cit.*, p. 69. Compare this determinist view of Foster's with Lenin's argument against the economists: "The Social-Democrat's ideal should not be the trade union secretary, *but the tribune of the people,* who is able to react to every manifestation of tyranny and oppression, no matter where it appears, no matter what stratum of class of the people it affects; who is able to generalize all these manifestations and produce a single picture of police violence and capitalist exploitation; who is able to take advantage of every event, however small, in order to set forth *before all* his socialist convictions and his democratic demands, in order to clarify for *all* and everyone the world-historic significance of the struggle for the emancipation of the proletariat." Lenin, *What Is to Be Done?* (Moscow, 1969), p. 80. Italics in the original.

The postwar policy was an alliance with anti-cold war liberals out of power. The second was better than the first, but in both cases the ideology of the alliance was liberal.

It is true that within the party—among its members and close adherents—there was a renewed commitment to Marxism and to the idea of a socialist revolution after Browder was expelled. This had tended not to be true in the previous decade, and particularly during the brief period of the Communist Political Association, when many party members never abandoned their liberal views even within the Communist social milieu. The return to Marxism was a consequence of the new militance and the new sense of opposition to those in power, and it was particularly strong among party youth. It was reflected in renewed reading of the "classics"—Marx (*Capital*), Lenin (*What Is to Be Done?* and *Left Wing Communism*), Stalin (particularly on the national question and the later *Economic Problems of Socialism*), and Mao Tse-tung and Liu Shao Chi (*On Contradiction* and *How to Be a Good Communist*) [11]—as well as in attempts to develop the characteristics of "socialist man" through the struggle against white chauvinism and male supremacy.

[11] It is important to note that these classics were never presented or understood in their historical contexts as political as well as abstractly "theoretical" works whose purpose was to argue for particular policies in particular social situations. Instead, the writings of these leaders were picked through to find the arguments that supported the line of the party at the moment. In the large body of Marxist writings, support could be found for almost any position if ripped out of its original context. This the party "theoreticians" constantly did.

6/

THE PROGRESSIVE PARTY AND
OPPOSITION TO THE COLD WAR

The Communist Party in Europe and the United States

In Europe, World War II provided a framework within which the Communist parties could become mass parties of the working class—at least in Czechoslovakia, Yugoslavia, France, and Italy—while in the United States (and in Britain) the war and its aftermath undermined the Communists' hard-won positions of influence. This occurred even though all Communist parties had adhered to the Popular Front and had subordinated a socialist politics to a classless policy of unity against fascism. The reason parties so similar in ideology, organization, and their understanding of the revolutionary process had such different fates is not difficult to determine. In fact, it lies in the common determinism of the Communist parties in regard to making history, in their common refusal to make socialism vs. capitalism the central issue of working-class politics. In short, the Communist parties of Europe did better than those in Britain and in the United States not because they had a superior understanding of socialism and revolution, but because they were the beneficiaries of "outside forces"—just as the American Communists were the victims of those forces.[1]

[1] And so far, despite their ability to build mass parties, the Communist parties of France and of Italy have not done much better than the American party in leading the

When the Popular Front came to an end in Europe the Communist parties emerged as the true patriots and defenders of national integrity. This was true because in both France and Italy (and in Yugoslavia and Czechoslovakia) the Communists had been the main organized armed force to oppose the fascist invaders. The ruling classes of these countries were divided. Some collaborated with the occupying forces, others were opposed to the Germans. But as leaders during the prewar years, the European ruling classes, collaborators and patriots alike, were responsible for the war, the occupation, and national humiliation. And when the invaders came, the patriotic capitalists did not stay and fight, they went into exile. They did not become part of the underground but relied on the Allied forces—on the English and the Americans, or on the Russians—to defeat the enemy. Meanwhile, the Communist-led underground organized the anti-fascist resistance at home. In the process, the Communists not only became the popular heroes, but the underground movement—the patriotic resistance—itself took on a working-class character and provided the basis for postwar Communist strength.

In contrast, Communists in the United States (and in Britain) merely cooperated with the bourgeois liberal forces, which were the major organizers of the anti-fascist war. And far from creating a working-class resistance in tacit opposition to the timid or fascist capitalists, the Communists played the opposite role. They became the main agents of the liberals in suppressing labor and black militancy during the war. They led in advocating no-strike agreements and in opposing "radical" demands by Negro integrationists. Thus, when the war ended they had no special credentials as representing a true national interest, and they had lost much of their reputation as militants. They had not helped to explain the class character of patriotism, but had helped to strengthen a classless loyalty to the ruling class by making "national unity" their main slogan. This appeared to be a good idea during the war against the Nazis. Its limitations became apparent when national unity against the Russians became the main idea of the cold war.

After Browder was removed from leadership, and the Communist

working class to socialism. Fate could make them mass parties, but it could not make them revolutionary parties. That they will have to do themselves or others will have to do it.

Party adopted Foster's view that ''an inherent drive to world domination was the main characteristic of world imperialism'' (a view obviously closer to reality than Browder's), the party continued to operate as if building a socialist movement were a two-stage process. Now the initial stage was to build a cross-class alliance of ''democratic forces'' against *all* wings of ''monopoly capital.'' Such an alliance, Foster argued, would have to go ''beyond anything in Roosevelt's time.'' This alliance was for a broad third party of the people. ''First,'' Foster argued, ''the workers should enter into organized cooperation with the poorer farmers, the Negro people, with the progressive professionals and middle classes, with the bulk of the veterans.'' Second, ''this great political combination must be led by the workers, by the trade unions.'' [2] The Popular Front was dead, but it lived on. This time, however, it was to be made up only of those out of power.

With the beginning of the cold war in 1946, the Communists had already begun to come under attack as agents of the Russian enemy. These attacks were the domestic counterpart of the United States's aggressively expansionist postwar policies. The United States had emerged from the war as the only capitalist power capable of defending not only its own immediate foreign interests but the world capitalist empire as a whole. Italy, Germany, and Japan were defeated and stripped of their imperial holdings. France, England, and the other European Allied powers were exhausted from the war and heavily in debt to the American corporate ruling class. The war, with its alliance between the Soviets and the capitalist democracies and its appeals to democracy and self-determination, had naturally stimulated movements for national independence in the colonies even as it weakened the grip of the imperial powers. From the point of view of the world capitalist class, a grave threat of socialist revolution now existed throughout the world. To stop this, the Russians had to be constricted in their sphere of influence and the Communist movement had to be destroyed or, at least, stringently opposed at home and in the colonies.

Within the United States from 1946 to 1948 the government instituted a purge of federally employed ''potential subversives'' and es-

---

[2] Quoted in Joseph Starobin, *American Communism in Crisis, 1943–1957* (Cambridge, Mass., 1972), pp. 122–123.

tablished a list of ''subversive'' organizations as a basis for similar action in private industry. In the labor movement plans to purge the left were initiated. State and federal un-American activities committees worked successfully to isolate left-wing unions, to get Communists and pro-Communists blacklisted from the movie industry in Hollywood, and to drive Communists and ''radicals'' from the nation's colleges and universities. In 1948 the Communist Party leadership was itself indicted under the Smith Act, and in the next few years a number of ''spy'' trials, most notably the Hiss case and the Rosenberg trial, molded public opinion and created the impression of a Russian plot.

The party's postwar line consisted of opposition to the emerging cold war and of a return to militancy within the unions and the civil rights movement. Communist policy was to work toward the formation of an independent third party, a new antitrust people's party of peace. The forces deemed necessary for such a party included major CIO unions, progressive anti-cold war Democrats such as Henry Wallace and Senator Claude Pepper (Florida), their Republican counterparts, New York's Fiorello La Guardia and Senator Wayne Morse of Oregon, major civil rights organizations, and various other ''people's organizations.'' Clearly, such a party could not be anti-capitalist, much less self-consciously socialist, but it could be anti-cold war and pro-union.

But was such a party possible in 1946? And, if not, how should the party proceed? For a few months in 1946 and early 1947 it seemed as if major segments of the labor movement and a significant number of liberal Democrats might break away and support a third party movement. But the party's dependence on anti-socialist forces in the unions and on progressive Democrats and Republicans made it more and more necessary to be led by events and to trail after groups whose vanguard the party fancied itself to be. And this seemed to rule out a third party in 1948.

/ Henry Wallace and the Progressive Party

/ In 1946 Henry A. Wallace, Vice President and Secretary of Agriculture during Roosevelt's Administrations and then Secretary of Commerce, resigned in opposition to the cold war policies of the Truman Administration. After Wallace's resignation, A. F. Whitney of the Brotherhood of Railway Trainmen invited him to address the union convention. Whitney was hostile to Truman because of the President's threat to draft railroad workers during a recent strike. Condemning Truman for having "removed every progressive appointed by Franklin D. Roosevelt," Whitney declared that Wallace was now "available to lead a movement for sound and progressive government." [3] Similarly, Jack Kroll, director of the CIO Political Action Committee, supported Wallace; and Phillip Murray accepted a position as vice president of the Progressive Citizens of America, a newly formed coalition in which the Communists were strongly represented and which was to be a key organization in Wallace's decision to run as an independent in 1948.

Despite these and other indications of support for Wallace, the movement away from the Democratic Party was short-lived. One by one the leaders retreated. Murray resigned from PCA in 1947, shortly after the anti-Communist Americans for Democratic Action was formed. Whitney about-faced when Truman vetoed the anti-labor Taft-Hartley Act (it was passed over his veto). By October 1947 CIO-PAC, Senator Pepper, and James Roosevelt had made it clear that they would not support a third party movement. By December 1947, when Wallace announced that he would run as an independent for President, he had almost no organized support beyond the party and its satellites. The major groups that the Communists had believed necessary for a successful third party—old-line New Dealers, major CIO unions, Negro organizations—had all begun to make their peace with Truman and to support, or acquiesce in, the cold war.

Given these developments, and given the party's determination to avoid sectarian isolation (which was the reason for not making socialism a political issue in the postwar period), it would have seemed logical to expect third party plans to be abandoned. In September 1947, Jack Stachel, the party's educational director, wrote in *Political Affairs* (the party political magazine) that "if the new people's party does not develop in 1948 it will surely come into being later." At the same time, he told his readers, "it could be accepted as a fact that the Communists alone, even with their left supporters in the labor and people's movement, will not and cannot organize a third party." Indeed, Stachel

---

[3] Quoted in Karl M. Schmidt, *Henry A. Wallace: Quixotic Crusade 1948* (Syracuse, 1960), pp. 21–22.

added, "a genuine, broad, mass third party would be of such proportions that the Communists could not possibly dominate it even if they sought to." The main thing was to organize a massive coalition against "the trusts," Stachel insisted. "The third party movement, and even the Wallace for President movement, which is much broader than the third party movement," were seen by Stachel as only "the most advanced sectors of this developing coalition."

Stachel's insistence on the broadest possible movement was supported by Eugene Dennis, party national secretary, in a speech at Madison Square Garden. "We Communists are not adventurers," Dennis insisted. "We are not going to isolate ourselves. We never did and do not now favor the launching of premature and unrepresentative third parties and tickets. Such moves can only succeed," he concluded, "when they arise out of the collective decision and united action of a broad democratic and anti-war coalition." [4]

But even while the party leadership generally was cautious and opposed moving toward a third party on its own, it took steps to facilitate a new third party if conditions became right. Since the Communists had no visible politics of their own, but were simply trying to strengthen the left wing of the liberal coalition, which centered in the Democratic Party, they were reduced to a politics of maneuver and manipulation. Throughout most of 1947 the party continued to work within the Democratic Party and even presented its third party activity as a means of strengthening the liberal Democrats. Thus, Dennis in August wrote: "It is possible, actually possible, for a third party movement to facilitate the election of a progressive presidential ticket in 1948. Such a victory will be possible if . . . there can be a coalition candidate, backed by the independent and third party forces, *running as a Democrat*. To put it realistically, no matter how theoretical it may sound, this is the *only* way for the third party and pro-Roosevelt forces to ensure the defeat of the G.O.P. candidate in 1948." [5]

Working out this perspective was complicated and involved apparently contradictory activities, as events in California best illustrate. In June 1947, after returning to California from a Chicago meeting of

[4] *The Worker,* September 28, 1947.

[5] "Concluding Remarks at the Plenum," *Political Affairs,* August 1947, pp. 688–700, quoted in Starobin, *op. cit.,* p. 162. Italics in the original.

the Progressive Citizens of America (PCA), Robert W. Kenny set about organizing a statewide meeting of "Democrats for Wallace." Kenny had been California's attorney general until 1946 when he ran unsuccessfully against Earl Warren for governor. He remained a power in the Democratic Party and was also close to the left. His meeting in Fresno (July 19) drew more than 350 delegates from the state's twenty-three congressional districts and served as a kickoff for building an all-western bloc for Wallace within the Democratic Party.[6]

At the same time, Hugh Bryson, president of the Marine Cooks and Stewards, a left-wing CIO union, also returned from the Chicago PCA meeting but with a different goal. Bryson argued for the formation of a new independent party immediately because California law required that it be accomplished before March 1948 in order to be on the ballot that year and because obtaining the necessary 275,970 voter signatures would take time.[7] Bryson believed that his activity, building an Independent Progressive Party (IPP), would neither interfere with Kenny's activity nor preclude its success. He argued that California needed something like the American Labor Party of New York, which in fact had always supported the Democrats.

Of course, getting 275,970 valid signatures demanded concentrated and disciplined work, and only the Communists could deliver that, given the lack of a popular movement with its own politics. The signature gathering work took Communists away from their activity within the Democratic Party, and Kenny saw this as suicidal for the left. In August he met with William Z. Foster and argued for concentration on mobilizing Democrats for Wallace. Foster responded favorably by emphasizing the danger of a Republican victory in his speeches and by referring to the third party as a project for the future. Foster's view seemed to be the predominant one within the party. It was reinforced by the general reluctance among Communists and their left-wing allies in the unions to force an issue that would split the CIO and isolate the left.

---

[6] The account in these paragraphs is taken from Starobin, *op. cit.,* pp. 163–164.

[7] A new party could have been created with 27,597 signatures of Democrats changing their registration. This procedure was decided against because it would remove the "most advanced" Democrats from that party. Getting the larger number had the advantage of forcing canvassers to talk to a large number of voters about the issues and about Wallace.

Thus, Harry Bridges announced on Labor Day that his union would "support the progressive forces in the Democratic Party," although, like Foster, he said that "the evils of the two-party system cannot be tolerated for the rest of our lives"—leaving the period of toleration uncertain. Similarly, the ILWU executive board backed Kenny and urged "progressives" to rally around "the fight to revitalize the Democratic Party." [8]

While the issue in California seemed to center on whether or not to form the Independent Progressive Party, in New York it centered on the nature of the already established American Labor Party (ALP). That party had been formed in 1936 by New Deal unionists, Communists, and Socialists in order to bring rank and file Socialists—who would not vote the Democratic ticket—into the New Deal coalition.[9] The ALP had always endorsed the Democratic ticket. Although the left thought of it as an independent working-class party, the ALP had functioned to eliminate the last traces of independent class politics among workers in New York and to reduce them to an interest group under New Deal hegemony. The Communists' lack of understanding of this was reflected in a discussion by Simon W. Gerson in the October 1947 issue of *Political Affairs*.

Gerson wrote that it was true that "within the A.L.P. and the progressive labor movement there are people who wholeheartedly support the principle of a third party but are not convinced about the necessity for a third ticket now." At the recent ALP convention, and also at the New York State CIO convention, this issue had been resolved simply by not raising the question of an independent Wallace candidacy in 1948. "This was the only basis for keeping the ALP intact—specifically, it meant keeping the Amalgamated Clothing Workers and the United Auto Workers within the ALP, which would have been impossible had the Wallace for President issue been placed before the convention." Gerson's article, of course, revealed much more than he intended. It laid bare the Communists' subordination to the trade unionists who dominated the ALP and who were moving toward support of the cold war. This relationship was analogous to that of the German Social

[8] Quoted in Starobin, *op. cit.*, pp. 166–167.

[9] The idea for the ALP was as much Roosevelt's as anyone's. The purpose was to win workers in New York away from the Socialist Party.

Democrats to the trade unionists within the German party in 1914. In a way it was worse, since in 1914 all Social Democrats, including the trade unionists, nominally accepted Socialist principles and the party's anti-war professions. This made possible an open struggle within the party between Luxemburg and Liebknecht on one side and the trade unionists and party bureaucrats on the other. In 1947 within the ALP there could be no such struggle because the ALP had no Socialist principles to begin with and because the trade unionists were not even nominally committed to an independent class politics. The Communists could not appeal to principle; they could only be power brokers, and the power was all on the other side.

To all outward appearances, then, it appeared certain as late as October 1947 that there would be no third party in 1947. Yet two months later the Progressive Party was being organized and Wallace had agreed to run—after being deluged by Communist-organized delegations urging him to do so.

As had always been true in the past, this sudden change of line was not caused by a change in conditions within the country, nor was it the result of prolonged debate over strategy within the party. The abrupt change came about as a result of the Soviet Union's change of line in Europe. In early October 1947 the Communist Information Bureau (Cominform) was organized. Its initial manifesto strongly condemned the Marshall Plan (for rebuilding Western Europe) and declared that the greatest danger facing the working class at the moment was underestimating its own strength and overestimating that of the imperialist camp.

This development impelled the American party to action that it would otherwise have eschewed. At the CIO national convention in September, for example, the Marshall Plan was not explicitly endorsed, and the Communists supported the foreign policy statement that called for foreign aid to be given purely on the basis of need. This was a compromise, similar to the avoidance of any discussion of a third party, that enabled the left and the dominant Murray forces to co-exist. Now, however, the party moved to condemn the Marshall Plan within the unions it controlled, and it interpreted the formation of the Cominform to mean that a third party must be built regardless of the effect of such a move on its position in the CIO. Some party leaders might have been influenced in part by the substantial popular enthusiasm for Wallace and for the party itself that was still being manifested. In San Francisco and Oakland, for example, Communists got more than 30 percent of the vote in November 1947, and in Chicago the Progressive Party—the label Wallace adopted in 1948—polled 300,000. This vote reflected considerable support for the wartime alliance with the Soviet Union, and for the pro-labor and pro-civil rights stance of the Communists and the left. But the decision to push opposition to the Marshall Plan within the CIO and AFL and to urge Wallace to run on a third party ticket was a decision for the party to move ahead virtually on its own. Of course, the alliance of the left with the CIO leadership was crumbling in any case. Nevertheless, for the party to take the initiative in ending its alliances with organized labor and the liberal Democrats facilitated and hastened its own demise.

The story of the Wallace Progressive Party, once the Communists had succeeded in convincing a slightly wavering Wallace to run, was similar to other liberal or "radical" third parties. Lots of enthusiasm and indications of popular support in the early stages of the campaign. Strong attacks from those outside the party, and the taking over of much of the new party's platform by the major parties—in this case by the Democrats. And a clear and sharp decline by the time of the elections. Wallace ended up with only 1,156,100 votes. He ran well only in New York, where the already established American Labor Party managed to get him 510,000 votes. By the end of the campaign Wallace was distinguished from Truman—who won in a surprising upset over Thomas E. Dewey—mainly on the issue of foreign policy and to a lesser extent on defense of Negro rights. Wallace opposed the cold war, but his principled stand was turned against him because the Progressive Party was so narrowly based and so clearly dependent on the Communists. Without any other substantial organizational support, the Progressive Party was effectively smeared as a Communist—and Russian—front.

The small vote for Wallace and the even smaller vote for other Progressive Party candidates was a mortal blow to hopes for establishing a permanent third party. Wallace remained with the new party for a little more than a year, but then resigned after the Korean War began in June 1950. In 1952 the Progressives again went through the motions with San Francisco attorney Vincent Hallinan as their candidate, but his poll of 150,000 votes was the end.

Meanwhile, partly as a result of the formation of the Wallace party and of Communist opposition within the unions to the Marshall Plan, CIO officialdom moved to expel eleven "Communist-dominated" unions in 1949. Before this happened, the party had already lost some of its most influential supporters in the CIO—most notably Joe Curran of the NMU and Mike Quill of the Transport Workers—when it decided to push the Progressive Party in 1948. Now the ILWU, the Mine, Mill, and Smelter Workers, the Distributive Workers, Marine Cooks and Stewards, Farm Equipment Workers, and others were expelled. The eleventh and largest of the left-wing unions, the United Electrical Workers (UE), was spared expulsion by quitting the CIO, but it did so only because a rival, the International Union of Electrical Workers (IUE), had already been chartered and was raiding UE shops. In the long run, almost all of these left-wing unions collapsed or were absorbed by mergers with stronger unions. The ILWU survived, and the UE, which lost more than 300,000 of its 500,000 members to IUE, did, too, gradually making a comeback. So did the Distributive Workers (District 65). But, except for the UE, these unions were no longer left-wing, whatever the private sentiments of their leaders and staff. Indeed, in San Francisco the Longshoremen's Union has become the mainstay of the right-wing Democratic Party machine.

Final Collapse

The years immediately following the collapse of the Progressive Party were years of defensiveness and disintegration for the left in general. The Communists had relied heavily on liberal-left coalitions to carry out their activity and, of course, by 1950 these were all but gone. This was true even before the accelerated onslaught by such demagogues as Senator Joseph R. McCarthy and Representative Richard M. Nixon, who simply seized upon the existing premises of cold war liberalism and the oppressive climate that had already been created. As domestic hysteria increased, virtually none of those Democrats and liberals who had once participated with the left in the New Deal or the wartime alliance were willing to defend their own former activities and associations. Now, in an effort to prove themselves completely "loyal," but also as a consequence of their own cold war, liberals frequently outdid the right wing in their attacks on Communists and other critics of postwar American policies.

By this time the party had lost its sense of direction and had no means of defense except to appeal to the very liberals who were attacking it to uphold traditional civil liberties. These appeals were fruitless monologues for the most part and gained little support outside the ranks of the steadily dwindling left. The cold war at home succeeded in creating a cowed and passive population partly because the left had built its strategy on alliance with liberal leaders and union bureaucrats and had not established an independent political base. The abandonment of these alliances by liberals and union leaders finally revealed how limited and ephemeral were the Communists' accomplishments during the 1930s.

Ironically, despite McCarthy's success in terrorizing liberals, conservatives, and leftists alike, the domestic repression symbolized by his attacks actually delayed the ultimate crisis within the party. Defense of the party and resistance to McCarthyism occupied the thoughts and actions of party members during these years. In a period of contraction and defense there was little time or apparent need for thinking about a positive program or a new society. The defense against McCarthyism became an end in itself—a fight for survival—and coincidentally a defense of the liberal social order. It provided no opportunity, even if the party had wanted one, to expose corporate liberalism in the name of a better way of life. Only with the demise of McCarthy at the hands of President Eisenhower and the Army did recognition of the real crisis within the party become unavoidable.

By 1955, Communists and those close to the party's various front organizations became increasingly aware that they had no direction—no vision of a socialist United States other than that provided by Soviet life. And, of course, the party had no long-range strategy aimed toward a socialist transformation. This had been true for a long time, but it had never been so close to the surface of party life and so acutely apparent to many party members.

This growing awareness was well advanced by 1956 when the left was struck by Nikita Khrushchev's revelations about Stalinist terror (at the Twentieth Congress of the Communist Party of the Soviet Union), and then by the Russian army's invasion of Hungary to put down a popular revolt. Now, in addition to lacking a public vision of socialism, the party's private vision was shattered. The combination of a steady decline of party influence, post-McCarthy aimlessness, and disillusionment over the Twentieth Congress and Hungary reduced the Communists to the impotence of other socialist sects. For the first time since 1900 American left-wing socialists were on their own—not only without a coherent theory or vision but also without an organized movement.

As the American Communist movement disintegrated, another event only 80 miles away further undermined the theoretical basis of party hegemony over much of the left. The Cuban revolution, which achieved state power at the beginning of 1959, was the first socialist revolution to be won without the leadership of Communists. Indeed, in Cuba the Communist Party had opposed Fidel Castro and the July 26 movement until victory was almost at hand. The Cuban revolution, coming so soon after the general collapse of the party in the United States, made it clear that the Communist movement was not "the sole correct path for mankind," which Communist leaders, party members, and many others close to the party had self-confidently believed and asserted since 1917.[10] Thus, at the end of the 1950s the field was wide open, in a way that had not been true since 1919, for the emergence of new formations on the left.

[10] See, for example, Palmiro Togliatti, "The Sole Correct Path for Mankind," *Political Affairs,* vol. 21, no. 1 (January 1952), p. 12.

7/

THE NEW LEFT

/ General Characteristics

The "new" left was not long in coming. The Communist movement collapsed in 1956–57. Its front groups all but disappeared and the trade union movement was almost uniformly a bastion of cold war conservatism. Yet even before the end of the '50s there were signs of the reemergence of social militance and the beginnings of a new anticapitalist movement. This was especially true among blacks in the South, where desegregation struggles and the registration drives were germinating before 1960. But it was also true on campuses. Beginning with SLATE at Berkeley in 1957, new militant student groups were formed at several larger universities. And by 1959, as an outgrowth of the Socialist Club at the University of Wisconsin, the first neo-Marxist publication, *Studies on the Left,* appeared. At the time these developments seemed unrelated and were in fact largely unconnected; the idea of a new left had not yet emerged. It took the organization of the Student Nonviolent Coordinating Committee (SNCC) in 1960–61 and the Port Huron meeting of Students for a Democratic Society (SDS) in 1962 to provide the basis for a popular consciousness that a new left was coming into being.

As this new movement developed, it easily understood itself to be as fundamentally different from the old left in its politics as it was in its social composition. The Communist and Socialist parties had centered around the trade unions, immigrant national groups, and to a lesser extent around ghetto blacks in Harlem and Chicago's South Side. The white new left centered around college campuses, and the black militants who went to work in the rural South were also mostly college students. In style, as well as in their social situations and their age, the new leftists were different from the old. But even so, many of their underlying assumptions about social change were shared with the old left.

But if this can be seen in retrospect, it did not seem so at the time, nor was it reflected in the organizational forms of new left groups. All the old parties were highly structured, centralized, and usually disciplined organizations, with clear lines of decision-making and little or no initiative from the membership. The new left was above all a highly decentralized movement that put its emphasis, especially in its early years, on participatory democracy. That emphasis was in part a response to the narrow ideological politics and squabbles among old left sects, each of which was clearly incapable of creating a popular movement around its narrow constructs and historical marginality. Taken in its best light, the new left aversion to structure and lines of organizational responsibility flowed from the belief of many of its early leaders that diversity and equal participation were necessary to the process of arriving at a new and potentially popular "radicalism." But this formal anti-elitism did not always, or even usually, prevent de facto elites from developing. And since the process of decision making in Students for a Democratic Society and other groups was often mysterious, it certainly did not eliminate manipulation by the elites.

Even so, the promise of a new socialist politics followed in part from the new left's openness, from its relative honesty, and from its commitment to a public radicalism. As a popular movement that was always at least in some part protesting and opposing the proletarianization of its own members, the new left always contained anti-elitist and socialist tendencies alongside its elitist missionary tendencies. The experience and centrality of the civil rights movement, and after 1965 of the anti-war movement, greatly strengthened the tendency of new leftists to understand their activity as directed against capitalist society as a whole and tended also to lead them away from narrow interest-group politics. But, especially before 1965, when anti-war activity pitted the new left against both the Democratic and Republican parties, the new left's politics remained cloudy.

Largely because it was spontaneous, because the process was not yet understood and almost all new radicals still thought (and, indeed, still think) in the prevailing sociological categories, there was a constant tension within the new left. The tension was between those who felt the need for a new society for their own sake, and who therefore saw themselves and others of the same social stratum as a legitimate component of a revolutionary movement, and those who saw themselves as members of a privileged middle class whose function as "radicals" was to organize the truly oppressed or simply to support their struggles. This tension has expressed itself in different ways. In SDS it first took the form of a conflict over whether to emphasize building a mass student movement on campuses or to use the student base for the "real" work of ghetto and other community organizing. Later it took the form of whether to move toward an explicitly socialist politics or to build an anti-imperialist movement in support of the Vietnamese and other colonial liberation movements. More recently it has expressed itself as a conflict between understanding the working class as diversified and stratified, capable of being unified only on the basis of opposition to capitalism and the need for socialism, and seeing the working class as a separate social grouping of blue-collar workers who have to be organized around their immediate needs as a prerequisite to raising larger political questions.

Underlying this tension were conflicting ideas about the revolutionary class and process. Most new leftists naturally thought in liberal pluralist categories, since these ideas permeated their own formal and informal education and were also prevalent in the Communist and Socialist parties. At first the major expression of this interest-group pressure politics was the search for a key revolutionary agent or constituency, and later, as the new left began to understand itself as socialist, in a narrow definition of the working class (as "blue-collar" workers) that excluded themselves. The idea that the most oppressed social group, or, later, the industrial workers, were the agents of revolution fit in with a missionary style of politics, with feelings of guilt on the part of most new leftists because of their own relative wealth and greater education, and with an understanding of "radicalism" as militant interest-group activity. In this latter respect, except that new leftists tended to downgrade the importance of the working class, new left and old left political practice was fundamentally the same: social mobilization around immediate interests, with the larger (revolutionary) consciousness remaining the private preserve of the organizers and activists.

Civil Rights

From the vantage point of the middle 1970s, the civil rights movement of the early 1960s can be seen as an attempt by blacks, with the partial and often reluctant support of liberal corporate groups, to end their isolation and be integrated more fully into the working class. Blacks fought for the rights earlier won by white working people, rights that characterize liberal capitalist society—public education, equal access to all public facilities, and the right to vote.

From the blacks' point of view these were simply demands for their human rights, which they have been denied because of their race. Radicals and most old leftists often saw these demands as revolutionary, in themselves a threat to the fabric of American capitalism. But within the logic of capitalist development these rights were a necessary part of integrating a rural, semifeudal work force into the capitalist marketplace. Blacks fought for their rights in the South, and to a lesser extent in the North, primarily out of immediate need and for their own dignity. Radicals fought partly out of a sense of guilt and from a moral conviction in the rightness of equal rights, but also because they believed this activity to be inherently radicalizing. Liberal politicians and corporate groups supported these struggles in order more fully to rationalize and integrate the labor market and also in the hope of reducing overt social conflicts—and the embarrassment that open racial oppression in the United States caused American policymakers in international affairs, especially in the face of the emergence of the newly independent African nations.

There are many ways of understanding when the civil rights movement began and what caused it. From the liberal corporatist point of view, the 1954 decision of the Earl Warren Supreme Court (*Brown* v. *Board of Education*) was the beginning of a new era in race relations. For the new leftists, the turning point in the movement was the series of sit-ins throughout the South that started at a lunch counter in Greensboro, North Carolina, on February 1, 1960.[1] For southern blacks (as, of course, for those in the North), it was a continuing struggle for equal rights and opportunities within American capitalism, a struggle that has had its ups and downs since blacks were brought to the United States as slaves, and especially since the end of the Civil War, when their formal status changed to that of free laborers.

The court decisions of the early 1950s were signals that provided new opportunities for dramatizing the struggle and these were seized upon almost immediately. The Montgomery bus boycott, led by Martin Luther King, began in late 1955. The Little Rock school struggle occurred in 1957 when President Eisenhower brought in federal troops to protect black students and to prove before the world that the United States stood for equality. By 1959, in Monroe, North Carolina, the struggles of the previous few years for equal treatment had been put down so brutally that Robert Williams of the NAACP began calling openly for armed self-defense.

Yet the lunch counter sit-ins in 1960 did signal the beginning of a new stage of sustained mass public activity in behalf of civil rights—activity that was to focus in the South for only a few years and would help trigger both the student movement and the nationalist ghetto movement in the North. The wave of sit-ins, soon to be followed by the 1961 "freedom riders" (organized by the Congress of Racial Equality—CORE), brought to a head feelings about the need for new tactics and, therefore, criticism of the older civil rights leaders in the Southern Christian Leadership Conference (SCLC).

The new left proper grew out of a widely shared need among student activists for organizations that "they could control and direct and which would not be subject to the authority of anyone but themselves." [2] The need was decisively expressed at a Southwide Student Leadership Conference in Raleigh, North Carolina, during Easter week of 1960. Martin Luther King and other SCLC leaders then tried to convince the students to form a student branch of SCLC. Instead they began

---

[1] See, for example, J. Kirk Sale, *SDS* (New York, 1973), p. 23. Sale refers to this incident as "The birth of the civil rights movement . . . ."

[2] James Forman, *The Making of Black Revolutionaries* (New York, 1972), p. 217. Forman presents a full account of SNCC's origin.

organizing a Student Nonviolent Coordinating Committee (SNCC), which was formally established in October of that year.

The goal of SNCC at the time of its formation was expressed by Ella Baker, an early leader of black students. Whatever differences students had in approaches to their goal, she wrote, "Negro and white students, North and South [were] seeking to rid America of the scourge of racial segregation and discrimination—not only at lunch counters, but in every aspect of life." [3] As stated, the goal was entirely consistent with that of the older civil rights groups, but the mood and the commitment to popular action that underlay Baker's statement was new. In their hearts, and in their private conversations, many of the new activists from the beginning questioned whether integration into the existing society was a sufficient goal—whether their purpose should not be larger. But the people they were trying to organize and serve clearly had no larger conscious goal. And the organization they had just created, SNCC, had emerged simply around the immediate need. It was never possible to spend time discussing the larger purpose of their work, even though many people in SNCC were aware of the contradiction between the actual meaning of their work and their own underlying purpose and desires. This can be seen clearly in relation to SNCC's activity in the area of voter registration, which was to be SNCC's major focus from 1961 to 1965.

For southern blacks the drive to register and vote during the early 1960s was similar to the drive among workers in the mass production industries for industrial unions in the 1930s. And in some ways the role of SNCC, although much less politically coherent, was similar to that of the Communist Party in that earlier time. SNCC's greatest achievement was its role in the voter registration drives in Mississippi, Georgia, and other states. SNCC organizers worked selflessly alongside rural southern blacks in conditions of poverty and of constant danger. Often their lives were immediately threatened, and always they were vulnerable to arbitrary and wanton violence.

For southern blacks, registering to vote, and voting, was a way of reducing their powerlessness. Those who have long had the vote and have seen countless liberals and populists get elected on radical plat-

[3] Quoted in *ibid.*, p. 218.

forms only to serve the existing powers, often see participation in electoral politics as having only marginal significance. Sometimes voting and running candidates is even viewed with hostility, as part of a fraudulent system designed to create the illusion of meaningful participation. But for blacks, voting was a means to challenge the arbitrary power of elected county officials. And the white racist sheriffs, other county officials, and members of the White Citizens' Councils understood and accepted the challenge. They threatened, and frequently attempted to kill, blacks who were trying to organize registration drives. And they often succeeded in terrorizing large numbers of blacks, especially in the early 1960s before the registration drives gathered momentum.[4]

Clearly, it would have been self-defeating for any organization that thought of itself as revolutionary not to participate actively and fully in the registration drives of the early 1960s. This is not simply because that was where the action was. More important, the registration drives and the idea and fact of voting brought blacks into collective political activity and out of their isolation. It not only made them less vulnerable to abuse by white employers and landlords, it also gave them a way to begin taking initiative as an underclass. But what use they would make of the vote, what kind of political activity they would move toward, was crucial to the meaning of the registration drives.

Some SNCC workers understood that there was an important, even a vital, issue here. As James Forman, a leader of SNCC, has commented, SNCC was "interested in trying to register voters so as to expose the dirt of the United States and thus alienate black people from the whole system," while "the United States, through the Kennedy Administration, was interested in trying to register voters for the sake of the Democratic Party." To achieve this exposure, working in the rural areas was important because it was there that "fear of the sheriff and the Ku Klux Klan, together with the desire of the whites to hold on to their power," was most obvious. Voter registration in rural areas "could create more exposure and thereby more consciousness."[5] Mass consciousness of the capitalist values that are predominant in the United

---

[4] See *ibid.*, Ch. 36, and *passim* for descriptions of the determination of local blacks and the terror they faced.

[5] *Ibid.*, p. 265.

States, and a rejection of these values by young black people, "would usher in revolutionary change," Forman believed.[6]

In large part, SNCC hoped to create this consciousness by setting an example, by demonstrating in practice its members' commitment to human values as opposed to the simple "making of money." SNCC workers were "not driven by the profit motive which dominates this society," and being against it "placed them against capitalism," at least in their own minds. They were willing "to build a community of brothers and sisters who would take care of each other insofar as possible," a community that could demonstrate "by the way in which its members lived that it stood against capitalism." As Forman observed, there were no other mass organizations doing this. Union organizers (particularly Communists) had often set such examples in the 1930s, but "the labor movement, which ought to be against [capitalism], had become part and parcel of the system in many ways." [7]

Unfortunately, SNCC's understanding of how the labor movement had become part of the system was superficial. It was, Forman insists, the high salaries that labor leaders received that made them less militant: "When a person becomes high-salaried there is a general tendency for him to become more interested in getting that salary than in the cause for which he is working." [8] But the question is rarely if ever a question of the degree of militance. Rather it is the nature of the cause, or, more important, the purpose of the activity that is crucial. And the high salary is only a symptom of acceptance of the capitalist system and its values. Communist organizers in the CIO during the 1930s did not need high salaries because they were motivated by a desire to build a revolutionary movement. But others in the CIO did not share that goal. They wanted only an organization that could get higher wages for workers within capitalism. That, after all, is the purpose of trade unionism within capitalism. And since it is, why should a trade union leader not share that purpose and avail himself (or herself) of that opportunity when it is won?

The Communists might have prevented business unionism from

---

[6] *Ibid.*, p. 237.
[7] *Ibid.*, pp. 236–237.
[8] *Ibid.*

taking over the CIO or might have at least built and sustained a political struggle for socialism while they served as organizers of the unions. But they believed that the trade union struggle itself, militant workplace activity, was sufficient—especially if the various organizers set examples as self-sacrificing militants not motivated by moneymaking values. However, a trade union that is not constantly challenged from the outside by a party that raises the question of socialist values and working-class political power must end up accepting capitalist values and cannot oppose the subordinate position of the working class within corporate capitalism.

The analogy to SNCC is obvious. SNCC did not see the need to be part of a larger socialist movement. Many SNCC organizers were motivated, initially at least, only by the immediate situation of blacks. Others accepted the prevailing notions, long practiced by both Communists and Socialists, that the need for socialism should not itself be made a public issue. Others believed entirely in spontaneous development and in setting personal examples of moral behavior. And, in any case, as Forman writes, "Working in the rural South, facing constant death, trying to heighten consciousness, seemed in itself an ideology around which all could rally." Developing a socialist politics, and especially becoming part of a larger movement, appeared hopeless (and probably was) at the time. There was too much work that needed to be done to spend endless hours in trying to reach political agreement. So, by common agreement, SNCC's position remained focused on the immediate situation. "Black people in the United States suffered from racism, from political and economic exploitation, and there was no mass organization fighting to change these conditions, especially in the rural areas of the country. SNCC had to play this role. If you were willing to work to change these conditions, then you subscribed to the broad, general ideology upon which the organization rested." [9]

As long as both the Republican and Democratic parties opposed the immediate demands of southern blacks (and of SNCC), it did remain possible for SNCC to limit itself to the issue at hand and at the same time to appear, both to its own members and to much of the American public, as revolutionary. It stood opposed to the dominant institutions

[9] *Ibid.*, p. 239.

and political organizations in American society. But when "the problems of voter registration and segregation of public accommodations were largely resolved with the passage of the 1964 and 1965 Civil Rights acts," the situation became confused. Then, Forman recalls, "our long-range goals, the kind of society we wanted to see built, the question of whether the fundamental problem facing black people was strictly racism or a combination of racism and capitalism, the role of whites—all these issues had to be dealt with and failure to do so tore the organization apart." [10] And now, of course, SNCC is gone and the Democratic Party remains.

The Student New Left

But in 1960, the example set by the freedom riders and the students who organized SNCC and began registering voters in Mississippi was positive and inspiring for young people in all parts of the country. This was especially so for Students for a Democratic Society (SDS) which was close to the freedom rides and the initial activity of SNCC. SDS had its formal beginning in January 1960, when the Student League for Industrial Democracy (SLID) changed its name to be more in tune with the times.[11] At its first conference, held at Ann Arbor in May 1960, the renewed civil rights activity in the South was clearly uppermost in people's minds. Billed as a conference on "Human Rights in the North," the SDS meeting was attended by Bayard Rustin, James Farmer of CORE (a former full-time SLID organizer), Herbert Hill of the NAACP, and representatives of SNCC. Early SDS leaders, Bob Ross, Al Haber, and Tom Hayden, were also present. The coincidence of the freedom rides and the reorganization of SDS helped both groups but was especially important in giving SDS its initial élan and direction. Less inspiring (and soon to be at least informally repudiated) but also important in getting it going were SDS's formal connection to the

---

[10] *Ibid.*

[11] SLID itself had been around for almost forty years, during which time its politics were similar to those of the Socialist Party. SLID, in turn, had its earliest origins in the Inter-collegiate Socialist Society, organized in 1905 by Jack London and others. At its height, before the United States entered World War I, the old ISS had about eighty chapters at various colleges and universities. It was then formally independent but was closely identified with the Socialist Party.

League for Industrial Democracy and a grant of $10,000 from the United Automobile Workers of America. The grant made it possible for SDS to hire Al Haber as its full-time field secretary, and thus to establish a national organization in a still difficult time for the left.

From its inception, under Haber's guidance, SDS was a departure from the cold war politics of SLID and its adult affiliates. To young socialists, like those in *Studies on the Left* and in other groups not tied to official liberalism or to the Norman Thomas, Michael Harrington anti-Communist left, SDS was a refreshing change. As Herschel Kaminsky recalls, SLID had always represented the "worst State Department kind of socialism." To meet someone like Haber, who was "talking about turning what had been SLID into a multi-issue organization that did more than just attack the Soviet Union was a surprise." And it was a pleasant one.[12] But it is important to remember that despite the new departure, SDS, like SNCC, had many connections to the old left, both in terms of its initial membership and in its organizational support. Several leaders of both organizations had been in or close to not only SLID, but also the Communist Party youth organization, the Labor Youth League (LYL). Nor were SDS and SNCC unique in this. Many participants in other independent groups had old left connections, either organizational or through their parents. This was true of new left publications as well, especially of *Studies on the Left,* many of whose initial editors had been members of either LYL or the Communist Party.[13]

SDS and SNCC were to be the major national organizations of the new left, but SDS grew very slowly until the Port Huron convention in 1962, and from Port Huron until the 1965 March on Washington it remained a relatively small part of the student movement as a whole. Many ad hoc groups sprang up from Berkeley to Cambridge in the early 1960s, mostly around immediate issues—such as the Caryl Chessman execution in California, the 1960 HUAC hearings in San Francisco, the plight of union miners in Hazard, Kentucky. Some of these formed into temporary organizations that followed one another as the central issues changed—SLATE, then the Free Speech Movement (FSM), then the

[12] Quoted in Sale, *op. cit.,* p. 29.

[13] For a description of the development of *Studies on the Left,* see James Weinstein and David W. Eakins, *For a New America* (New York, 1970), Introduction.

Vietnam Day Committee (VDC) at Berkeley. In addition, starting with *Studies on the Left*, several new student magazines appeared: *New University Thought* at Chicago, *Root and Branch* at Berkeley, and others at Cornell University, the University of North Carolina at Chapel Hill, and elsewhere.

All the various groups were motivated by the idea of democracy and equality, captured in the SDS slogan of "participatory democracy." The president of the SLATE Peace Committee, arguing for Easter peace demonstrations in 1960, insisted that "the power of democracy is a living idea" and that "freedom of speech, equality, self-determination of peoples" were "the most powerful political ideas in the world." [14]

But if this is true, why would a radical student left arise in the United States, the most democratic nation in the world, in a period when the remnants of McCarthyism were receding into the background? And why would the new left be almost entirely a student movement, when students were relatively well off and traditionally a part of the ruling or middle classes—and, therefore, already "participants" in the decision-making process? The answer was in part ideological. It lay in the glaring discrepancy between the prevalent cold war celebration of American success and freedom and the reality of systematic poverty and powerlessness experienced by millions of Americans, especially blacks. And, later, of course, the imperial role of the United States, especially in Vietnam, became increasingly clear, as did the hypocrisy and brutality of the policies of corporate leaders and their Republican and Democratic politicians.

But cold war ideology was only one aspect of the post–World War II policies designed to prevent a return to the crisis of the 1930s. And moral indignation was only one aspect of the new left's experience—although always an important one. Changes in the meaning of higher education, and in the role and class position of college-educated labor, were at least as important, although these were much less clearly understood throughout the 1960s.

The Great Depression had lasted more than ten years and was ended only as a result of massive arms expenditures by the government

[14] Quoted in Massimo Teodori, ed., *The New Left: A Documentary History* (Indianapolis, 1969), p. 122.

along with the absorption of surplus workers into the armed services during World War II. That experience had finally made it clear to the decisive majority of corporate leaders that the operation of the ''free market'' could no longer provide sufficient investment opportunities or enough jobs in industry for workers displaced by increasing productivity. To maintain a satisfactory level of profits and employment, government intervention was necessary on a massive scale, both to protect and subsidize private capital.

In the early 1940s economists almost universally anticipated a postwar return to depression. It was to prevent that return that the government (with the aid and advice of corporate planners) embarked on a series of programs, with the cold war at the center. Under cover of a battle between godless Communism and the ''Free World,'' the United States assumed global responsibility for the maintenance of empire and justified a policy of massive armaments spending (creating jobs and profits without dumping goods on the market). For a time, the cold war ideology also hid the changed nature of American imperialism after World War II. Before the war, although the United States was as involved in overseas trade and investment as were other capitalist nations, it had few colonies and generally opposed colonialism in the interest of ''free trade'' or the Open Door—a policy that allowed American corporations to compete, more or less freely, in the markets of ''sovereign'' nations like China or Argentina. After the war, when American corporations pushed for vastly expanded overseas investment for their surplus capital, the United States was the only nation with the power to reimpose the colonial system throughout the world. Germany and Japan were defeated; England, France, and Holland were exhausted and had to rebuild their domestic economies. Only the United States emerged with a vastly expanded productive capacity and the will to take responsibility for capitalist survival throughout the world. So, for example, in 1945 the United States decided to support France's return to Indochina and for the next nine years provided the great bulk of military supplies used in the unsuccessful attempt to reestablish French colonialism in Vietnam. And when France failed even with that aid, the United States stepped in to prevent the escape of the Vietnamese from imperial domination.

Within this overall situation, the position of youth and the meaning of being a college student was also rapidly changing. In 1940, just before the war, only 12 percent of 18- to 20-year-olds were in college.[15] By 1970 about 50 percent were enrolled. This vast increase in the student population served two purposes: to delay entry into the work force of several million youth for several years and to train millions of new workers, no longer needed in the direct production of goods, for jobs in sales promotion and service, social control, administration, and various kinds of research and development. The meaning of being a college student and the nature of the work that college-trained people did after graduation changed dramatically with the rapid expansion of higher education. Students, most of whom two decades earlier were from or were entering the middle class (small entrepreneurs, independent professional, upper-level management), now, by and large, were faced with becoming employees in corporate or government bureaucracies.

The knowledge industry, as Clark Kerr of the University of California correctly called it, had become both a "prime instrument of national purpose" and a vast new training ground for new kinds of workers. In Kerr's words, "What railroads did for the second half of the nineteenth century and the automobile for the first half of this century, the knowledge industry may do for the second half of this century: that is, to serve as the focal point for national growth." [16] And just as the railroad and automobile industries had created new groups of workers, so would the university (although, of course, the university did not produce material goods, but only skills, ideology, and ideologues).

This new function of the universities—to produce a new kind of worker, in contrast to their earlier function of training professionals and culturally sophisticated businessmen—did not meet the expectations of many students, especially at the more elite schools. Traditionally, places like the University of California at Berkeley were training grounds for the thinking elite of American society. This was still so to a substantial degree in the 1960s. But the students at Berkeley and other elite schools also were the ones with the highest expectations, and they were thus highly sensitive to their approaching proletarianization. What

[15] Robert Carson, "Youthful Labor Surplus in Disaccumulationist Capitalism," *Socialist Revolution*, no. 9 (May–June 1972), pp. 35–36.

[16] Quoted in Sale, *op. cit.,* p. 22.

this meant to students and how some of them felt about it was most clearly expressed by Mario Savio of the Free Speech Movement at Berkeley in 1964.

Savio, whose charisma consisted of explaining to students the underlying causes of their dissatisfaction, was himself not a socialist and did not think of himself as a revolutionary. In this respect, of course, he was like the vast majority of students. His experience was different mainly in that he had worked with SNCC in Mississippi the previous summer. He had gone there to "join the struggle for civil rights," and his activity in FSM that fall in Berkeley was understood by him to be "another phase of the same struggle." Mississippi and Berkeley were two battlefields where the same rights were at stake: "the right to participate as citizens in a democratic society and the right to due process of law." As Savio explained, the university in the postwar period had become "part and parcel of this particular stage in the history of American society; it stands to serve the needs of American industry; it is a factory that turns out a certain product needed by industry or government." That product was supposed to be an unthinking and unquestioning cog in a vast bureaucratic system. "The 'futures' and 'careers' for which American students now prepare," Savio complained, were, "for the most part, intellectual and moral wastelands." But Savio was determined to help fight for a future in which men and women would not be "standardized, replaceable, and irrelevant." [17]

The commitment to engage in "active dissent" against social inequality and for democratic participation in political life was the common bond among early new leftists. Through it the new left broke both with the liberal celebration of the status quo and with the paralyzing sectarian in-fighting of the old left and provided a sense of community among activists throughout the country. The best expression of the new activism, the Port Huron Statement of SDS (1962), stressed these ideas and affirmed the human "potential for self-cultivation, self-direction, self-understanding, and creativity." This was to be the best side of the new left.

The authors of the Port Huron Statement also insisted that a "first task of any social movement is to convince people that the search for

[17] Mario Savio, "An End to History," Teodori, *op. cit.*, pp. 159–161.

orienting theories and the creation of human values is complex but worthwhile.'' [18] However, it was not consciously through theory but in unselfconscious activity around their ''feelings'' on issues that radical students soon began to see the limitations of liberal ''solutions'' to the evils they opposed. Thus, for example, the growing awareness of the systematic oppression of blacks not only in the South but also in the northern ghettos made people question what good the simple attainment of civil rights could do. As one early SDS community organizer observed, '' 'civil rights' gets the Negro in the South no more than a Harlem.'' [19] And events in the early 1960s combined to reveal the inhuman nature of corporate capitalism at a time when liberal ideologues were busy crowing over the virtues and triumphs of the system. For example, the invasion of Cuba by CIA-trained and -financed counterrevolutionaries in 1961—and the exposure of the bald lies of Adlai Stevenson and others in denying complicity—undermined people's faith in the liberals' professions of support for democracy abroad.

This apparently ''natural'' process of radicalization reinforced the dominant pragmatism of the movement, even while it pushed the new radicals to the left. And the new left's pragmatism strengthened the tendency toward interest-group politics. In these early years of the new left, socialist theory, in which the working class is central, fell into disrepute among most sections of the movement because students saw themselves as ''middle class'' and saw workers and their unions as a mainstay of the cold war and of racism.

The narrow and conservative trade-unionist politics of both the Socialist and Communist parties helped bring the new left to look upon socialism, as well as the old parties, as irrelevant. And it also helped to reinforce the other strand within the new left, its elitism, which was implicit in its social position and explicit in much of its politics from Port Huron until the present. In the Port Huron Statement, SDS argued that the university was central to ''social change,'' in part because ''any new left in America must be, in large measure, a left with real intellectual skills, committed to deliberativeness, honesty, reflection as working tools.'' This was true enough, but its meaning to the young student

[18] Quoted in Teodori, *ibid.,* p. 166.
[19] Carl Whitman, ''Students and Economic Action,'' *ibid.,* p. 128.

radicals was ambiguous. In part, it meant building a mass movement for "radical social change" on the campuses, among people whose immediate experience was already radicalizing them. This new movement could not change society itself but could act as a catalyst to "awaken its allies, and by beginning the process towards peace, civil rights, and labor struggles, reinsert theory and idealism where too often reign confusion and political barter." [20] This view implied a multi-sectoral politics in which the student movement constituted one part. The student movement was to be built around the immediate experience of college, but it had to be infused with the understanding that a movement of many sectors of the population was needed. Understood this way, Port Huron was an anticipation of the "new working class" theories of 1966–67.

But the university was also seen as the place where a necessary social elite was formed, one that could involve itself in "uncomfortable personal efforts" that those who had to "rely on aching stomachs to be the engine force" of action were not prepared to undertake.[21] This elitist concept of social change was strengthened by the rejection of socialist class theory and by the unquestioned acceptance of prevailing bourgeois sociological categories, in which college students were defined as middle class by their life-styles, income levels, and educational attainments. In the absence of a Marxist conception of class, such an understanding obviously made sense because students and especially the student activists were generally from higher income families, had "middle class" life-styles, and were among the best educated members of American society. This contradiction between democratic and non-elitist goals and a missionary sense of helping those less well off was the basis of much political ambivalence in the new left.

Within SDS, at least from Port Huron (1962) to the anti-war March on Washington in April 1965, political ambivalence took the form of disagreement over whether the organization should concentrate on building a mass radical student movement on campus or should serve primarily as a support group for the small number of SDS members who were trying to organize "community unions" of the ghetto poor. In part, SDS's problem arose from the fact that it was trying to be a radical

---

[20] Quoted in Teodori, *op. cit.*, pp. 171, 172.
[21] *Ibid.*

student movement when the country had no organized left. Thus, while the Port Huron Statement saw the university as "a potential base and agency in a movement of social change," it was not long before SDS leaders began asking how universities, designed to train leaders and ideologues for the existing system, could be the basis of a movement for fundamental change. Obviously, a revolutionary movement could not exist only in the universities, since the universities themselves were clearly not the sources or center of power in society.

This insight—that while the university was generating a left op-position, it was still very much a functioning and integrative part of capitalist society—could have led SDS to understand itself as one part of the process of building a revolutionary movement among all sectors of society. And, indeed, Tom Hayden did argue that "the university cannot be reformed without a total social revolution." [22] But he did not do so in order to promote a movement (much less a party) of several different sectors. He did not argue that SDS must seek to build a broader movement, with itself as the student arm. Instead, entirely within the framework of old left pragmatism, Hayden sought another key social grouping to organize, one that would more "naturally" lead in a revolutionary direction.

That group was the ghetto poor. In 1963 this was a natural choice because the organized industrial workers were quiescent, apparently satisfied with their lot, while the unions were very much a part of the system. Poverty, on the other hand, had just been "rediscovered." And thus Hayden argued that working in poor communities was a "position from which to expose the whole structure of pretense, status, and glitter that masks this country's real human problems." Furthermore, working among the ghetto poor in the North was as close as SDS could get to emulating SNCC's activity among the southern rural poor. Thus Hayden, himself at the very center of this new movement, could be unself-conscious—or dishonest—enough to opine that "The Movement is a community of insurgents aiming at a transformation of society led by the most excluded and 'unqualified' people." Missionary self-deception aside, Hayden argued that to be relevant, SDS had to drop its concentration on campus organizing and go to the *people*, to the ghetto poor. In

---

[22] Quoted in Sale, *op. cit.,* p. 86.

the ghetto, Hayden argued, SDS could listen to the people, "learn from them, organize them to demand from society the decent life that is rightfully theirs," and thus be engaged in revolutionary activity.[23]

In making this argument, Hayden took the "key sector" idea from the old left (although with the poor rather than the industrial workers as the "key") and played upon the worst characteristic of the new left, its guilt, which was based on acceptance of the idea that it was a "middle class" movement with no legitimate self-interest in a revolutionary transformation of capitalist society. Hayden also expressed a widely shared impatience with SDS's limited activity on campus and its lack of a clear program. Being relevant politically was a legitimate need of SDS members, and the way to be so as a purely campus organization was unclear. Action, any action, appeared better—and probably was better—than remaining solely on campus with no clear purpose. Thus Hayden's argument for the new direction was overwhelmingly approved.

The ghetto organizing projects, done under the name of the Economic Research and Action Project (ERAP), never did involve large numbers of students at any given time. Perhaps two hundred people were actually organizers in some ten cities. Newark, New Jersey (NCUP—the Newark Community Organizing Project), Chicago (JOIN—Jobs of Income Now), Cleveland, Boston, and other smaller cities were the sites of the projects. Of these, NCUP and JOIN were the most elaborate, received the greatest resources, both financial and human, but shared the common fate of ERAP projects—failure by any reasonable criteria. Yet Hayden argued forcefully, and successfully for a year or two, that these projects should be the main activity of SDS and that campus chapters existed primarily to service ERAP projects. The projects themselves were elitist both in the sense of being missionary activities and in their internal structures. Under the guise of participatory democracy, the most articulate and manipulative personalities—Hayden in Newark, Rennie Davis and one or two others in Chicago—dominated the projects, which never had any clear politics or program. Women were especially victimized—to the extent, in Chi-

---

[23] *Ibid.,* pp. 101, 107. The latter quotation is of Sale's summary of Hayden's remarks.

cago, of being sent to work as sales clerks in Woolworth's in order to support the men as organizers when outside funds ran low. Indeed, these experiences were part of the early impetus for women's caucuses in SDS, which then became an early basis for the women's liberation movement in the late 1960s.

Some of the early SDS leaders had opposed ERAP's concentration on ghetto organizing—Haber most prominently. They had lost out and largely dropped out of activity between 1963 and 1965. But a campus-oriented tendency continued to exist, and as the ERAP experience became clear, it gradually gained strength. This process was accelerated by the Free Speech Movement (FSM) at Berkeley, which began as a protest against a ban on solicitation of funds for off-campus political action in September 1964, and finally won its battle in early January 1965. The FSM involved thousands of students in confrontation with the university administration and with the police. As a collective social action it far overshadowed the various ERAP projects. For the first time it made clear that the student movement could be a social force in its own right.

Clark Kissinger, then national secretary of SDS, but not one of the charismatic leaders, immediately grasped the potential in the FSM. Although Kissinger had not been elected as a representative of either side, he felt increasingly that SDS had to return its focus to campus activity. But to do so required a national focus for student work, which FSM did not provide. Where to find one?

8/

SDS AND VIETNAM

The answer came at the SDS National Council meeting in New York in late December 1964, even before FSM had won its struggle. Todd Gitlin and Paul Booth had invited the radical journalist I. F. Stone to the council meeting to tell the delegates how the United States had become involved in Southeast Asia. Stone gave a short history of American involvement in Vietnam and argued that the United States should withdraw its "advisers" from the war. Up to that time, most SDSers, like most Americans, were virtually unaware that the United States had been involved in a neocolonial war in Indochina. But the National Council delegates were moved by Stone's account, and Kissinger, Gitlin, and others saw in the war an opportunity for common action of the various SDS chapters. The campus-oriented delegates proposed and supported a national action against the war. The ERAP delegates opposed an anti-war action on the ground that it would take attention away from the community organizing projects. A third group, the smallest and closest to the anti-Communism of the LID (this group was led by Steve Max), did not oppose anti-war action but was concerned that it not be too leftist or appear to be pro-Communist. After hours of debate, and when several ERAP delegates were out of the room, Kissinger pushed through a proposal for an SDS-sponsored March on Washington in April.[1]

The march was designed to protest American involvement in Vietnam, but no specific programs or proposals were endorsed. There was a consensus that the war was bad, but none about what steps should be taken to disengage. But most SDS leaders disliked and opposed the cold war anti-Communism of the LID and the existing official peace movement—groups like the Committee for a Sane Nuclear Policy (SANE), Turn Towards Peace, and the War Resisters League (WRL). And not being ideological cold warriors, their natural sympathies went to the National Liberation Front in Vietnam, the organization of Vietnamese, North and South, which was conducting the struggle for Vietnamese independence. This created an underlying tension between SDS and the "adult" peace groups and leaders, one that soon led to open hostility and from there quickly to the transformation of the peace movement as a whole from one of ideological support for American policymakers to an oppositional force that began to understand itself as revolutionary.

Consistent with its "anti-anti-Communism," the SDS National Council decided that its march would not practice exclusion. SDS would be the sole sponsor, but any group that shared its purpose, which was to provide a focus for the rising student protest against United States' involvement in Vietnam, could join. During the first week of January 1965 invitations went out to all student political organizations and to all "adult" peace groups. These announced SDS's intention to hold a March on Washington on April 17, asked endorsement, and invited each group to appoint a liaison to help coordinate activity. The Du Bois Clubs (an organization close to the Communist Party) and the Young Socialist Alliance (the Socialist Workers Party youth arm) immediately endorsed the march and promised active participation. The May 2 Movement (which was close to Progressive Labor) did not officially endorse but indicated approval. The major peace organizations, SANE, WRL, Turn Towards Peace, Women's International League for Peace and Freedom, Student Peace Union, Fellowship of Reconcili-

---

[1] Hayden and other ERAP organizers opposed any potential diversion of attention and resources from their community projects. Even after the April march, Hayden argued at the 1965 SDS convention in Kewadin, Michigan, that SDS campus chapters should devote most of their energies to servicing NCUP and other projects.

ation, all ignored the invitation. A. J. Muste, an old-time radical pacifist, and David McReynolds of WRL asked to meet with the SDS leaders to discuss the date, which coincided with traditional Easter Saturday peace activity, and also the participation of the Du Bois Clubs. McReynolds was particularly unhappy with the political character of the march, and after the meeting neither he nor Muste offered endorsement or support.

Similar reactions came from other ''adult'' leaders, all of whom believed that SDS alone could not bring more than a few hundred diehards to Washington. Worried that this might be true, SDS leaders asked for a meeting with Bayard Rustin (who had organized three marches on Washington, including the August 1963 March for Freedom that brought 200,000 people to the Capital). The meeting was arranged and Rustin, along with Michael Harrington and Tom Kahn of LID, met with the SDS staff. Rustin, Harrington, and Kahn all objected to the march's style and political content, but Rustin promised to give unofficial assistance.

Then, on February 11, President Johnson announced the official beginning of massive bombing over North Vietnam. Rapidly the outlook for the march began to change. On scores of campuses it began to offer a needed means of national protest. Soon the old-line peace leaders also began to change their minds. They decided that the SDS project should become the national focus for spring activity against the war and that they should cancel their own activity and support the march. This change in plans was followed by negotiations with SDS to change the sponsorship from SDS alone to an ad hoc committee of SDS and the other organizations now involved, although it was unclear just what relation the ''left-wing'' (Du Bois Clubs, YSA, May 2) groups would have to the committee. At first SDS appeared to accept the arrangement, but after a referendum and some changing of votes, the proposal was rejected and SDS remained the sole sponsor. The final decision not to accept an ad hoc committee came after the adult groups had sent out their own call on the assumption that they were co-sponsors, and some felt that SDS had tricked them into giving full support. These leaders then withdrew and began criticizing and working against the march.

But the main objections that the old-line peace groups had were political. During the final weeks before the march this became clear in a series of outbursts against SDS. The first incident was a poster, prepared for advertisements in the subways (the advertising company refused to put them up), which stated that the United States was "burning, torturing, and killing the people of Vietnam" to "prevent free elections." This made many of the old-line people furious because, they said, the poster implied that if the United States withdrew free elections would follow. Next, SDS was attacked by Robert Pickus of the Western Area Turn Toward Peace, for activity that was "in fact more hostile to America than to war." The West Coast rally, timed to coincide with the Washington march, was jointly sponsored by the Du Bois Clubs, Women's Strike for Peace, and SDS. According to Pickus, the rally had to be opposed because it "would condemn American violence and ignore the use of violence by other forces in Vietnam." This was seen by Pickus, as it was by Lyndon Johnson, as "anti-American." [2]

Finally, several press releases and a song sheet issued by SDS also piqued various cold war peace leaders. One SDS press release argued that the march was a unique protest because it attempted to rouse an independent constituency not tied to the Johnson Administration. Another press release accused the President of attempting to "con the American people." The peace leaders were distressed that SDS opposed their traditional dependence on liberal Democrats and considered the personal attack on Johnson to be intemperate and tactless. As if to confirm these leaders' fears, SDS then released "Songs of Vietnam," a mimeographed sheet containing familiar songs with new words. One song was a revised "freedom song" with new words by Todd Gitlin. The verse began with "No strategic hamlets/ No strategic hamlets around me," and continued: "And before I'll be fenced in/ I'll vote for Ho Chi Minh/ Or go back to the North and be free." That was too much, the LID people complained. There was no freedom under Ho Chi Minh in the North. Unless SDS realized this and asserted the totalitarian nature of North Vietnam and other Communist regimes, the protest value of the Washington march would be dangerously compromised.

What that meant, so far as these adult leaders were concerned,

---

[2] This account is taken substantially from the editors, "The SDS March on Washington," *Studies on the Left,* vol. 5, no. 2 (Spring 1965), pp. 61–69.

became clear in the final days before April 17. On April 15, the SDS staff received a call from Senator Ernest Gruening (Democrat, Alaska) and from I. F. Stone. Gruening had been warned that the march might be "infiltrated" by Communists. Stone was worried that Gruening might decide not to speak at the post-march rally. Both were assured that SDS was in control, and both did speak.

That same afternoon, April 15, a dozen or more influential leaders of the peace movement met to discuss what to do about the march. The meeting was called by Rustin, who, according to A. J. Muste, wanted "to torpedo the march because he thought Communists had taken it over in some places." [3] Rustin wanted to issue a strong statement condemning the march, but after much discussion a milder statement was released. This, in turn, became the basis of an editorial red-baiting the march in the New York *Post* of April 17, the day it took place. The editorial commented that "several leaders of the peace movement have taken clear note of attempts to convert the events into a pro-Communist production." It then summarized the peace leaders' statement and warned that "there is no justification for transforming the march into a frenzied, one-sided anti-American show. Some of the banners advertised in advance are being carried in the wrong place at the wrong time."

The virtual repudiation of the march by the old cold war radicals and liberals was immediately followed by its phenomenal success—it drew 25,000 people, then a record-sized crowd for a peace demonstration. This, in turn, led to a break between the new student movement and the cold war socialist and peace groups that was soon formalized by the official separation of SDS from its parent LID in October 1965.

The decisive break with the old-line socialists created a new kind of radical politics. For the first time in the United States the leadership of both the revolutionary movement and the peace movement passed into the hands of students and youth. The war in Vietnam and the protest movement that SDS and other student groups organized against it from 1965 to 1968 pitted this new left against the liberal establishment,

---

[3] See Jack Newfield's interview with Muste, *Village Voice,* May 6, 1965, quoted in "The SDS March on Washington," *ibid.*

as well as against the conservatives. Standing against all representatives of corporate capitalism, the anti-war movement quickly came to understand not only that the system was undemocratic, corrupt, and immoral, but also that it was a *system*. But, at the same time, the new left's experience with the Socialists and Communists militated against the development of a socialist consciousness. To most new leftists, socialism remained a dogmatic, bureaucratic, "old-fashioned" idea. Thus, as new leftists became "revolutionaries"—came to understand that corporate capitalism had to be rejected—they had no concept of an alternative social system. In that situation, new left politics became increasingly negative. The form of its activity, rather than a comprehensive political perspective or a positive program, became a mark of how "radical" it conceived itself to be.

Both sides of this process were reflected at the April 17 march in a speech by Paul Potter, SDS president. Potter, as Todd Gitlin said later, was "pure SDS, he doesn't get it out of books—he has a remarkable ability to think for himself and not pay attention to all the rhetorical shit whether academic or political." Potter cried that the war in Vietnam provided "the terrifyingly sharp cutting edge that has finally severed the last vestige of illusion that morality and democracy are the guiding principles of American foreign policy." He then went on to ask: "What kind of a system is it that allows good men to make those kinds of decisions?" And he concluded that it was time to name that system, to "name it, describe it, understand it, and change it." [4]

But in characteristic SDS style, Potter failed to name the system, much less to say whether or not "radical social change" meant overthrowing capitalism in favor of socialism. While Potter was speaking about the need to name the system, people in the crowd shouted for him to say "capitalism" or "imperialism." But as he later explained, "I did not fail to call the system capitalism because I was a coward or opportunist." And given the courage it took to make his speech, that certainly appears to be true. Potter's refusal had a deeper cause, which lay in the prevalence of liberal ideology and the failure of the socialist left to develop an adequate analysis of corporate capitalism. As Potter explains, he failed to call capitalism capitalism because "for me

[4] See J. Kirk Sale, *SDS* (New York, 1973), pp. 187–188.

and my generation'' that was ''an inadequate description of the evils of America—a hollow, dead word tied to the thirties.'' [5]

Thus, despite the rapid spread of radical consciousness among students and a growing awareness that it was the system as a whole and not just particular issues that were at stake, the new left did not develop a strategy that posed the existing social structure against a new one. At this stage student radicals had no conception of themselves as part of a revolutionary (or potentially revolutionary) class, one that could speak for and in the name of a new society. Indeed, in the community organizing stage of SDS, when student radicals were asked ''What do you people want?'' (the inevitable but not misplaced question), they insisted that it was not their job to provide answers, but only to make it plain that changes were needed.

Most of the community organizers had a sense that they were building a ''mass radical movement'' with the intention to ''transform American institutions.'' [6] And yet they could argue that ''Poor people need to form independent movements if the war-on-poverty is to get anywhere,'' that, in general, ''even 'reforms' require millions of people taking direct action and organizing themselves.'' [7] Lacking an explicit socialist framework, that view fit perfectly within the pluralist schema of political science and within American corporate liberalism. Under competitive capitalism in the nineteenth century, political activity by an under-class was understood as a contest for power in the name of the class, but under corporate liberalism ''independent movements'' of workers or the poor serve simply as pressure groups for the winning of particular reforms within the system. To the extent that ERAP organizers taught poor people how to organize themselves as a pressure group to win reforms without simultaneously bringing them into a larger socialist movement to change the basic class relations of society, they served to strengthen the existing liberal pluralism. Thus, Frank Mankiewicz, then director of the Latin American operation of the Peace Corps, talked about Hayden's NCUP: ''The things SDS has done in Newark

---

[5] Quoted in *ibid*.

[6] Todd Gitlin, ''The Radical Potential of the Poor,'' in Massimo Teodori, ed., *The New Left: A Documentary History* (Indianapolis, 1969), p. 137.

[7] Tom Hayden and Staughton Lynd, ''Reply to Herbert Gans,'' *Studies on the Left*, vol. 5, no. 3 (Summer 1965), p. 136.

are valuable to be exposed to. We want to take advantage of their experience.'' [8]

And yet, the new left was not just another pressure group. For not only did the need for revolutionary change (albeit still undefined) become more and more widespread and explicit among people in the movement, but students were beginning to be seen as a legitimate social force in their own right, as part of a ''new working class'' that could fight for a new society in its own interest. Even though the new left analysis of revolution and of the class role of students was unclear, it contained a potential beginning for a new socialist politics in the United States.

The "New Working Class"

The anti-war movement spurred the development of a new understanding of the class position of students, since unlike the community organizing days, tens, maybe hundreds, of thousands of students were now engaged in activity on their own behalf. As SDS grew into a movement with hundreds of chapters and many thousands of members the need to understand this experience stimulated thinking about students as part of a ''new working class.'' This development at first centered around Bob Gottlieb, Dave Gilbert, and Gerry Tenney in New York and was further developed by SDS national officers Carl Davidson and Greg Calvert.[9] Its most advanced expression was in the attempt to build the movement among college (and often SDS) graduates—a Movement for a Democratic Society (MDS) and Teachers for a Democratic Society (TDS), both formed in 1968.

At its best, the new working-class theory was a way of understanding student activism and anti-war organization as part of a working-class movement against capitalism. From 1965 to 1968 anti-war activity seemed to pit the movement against all of the existing establishment and therefore against the system as a whole. Unlike ghetto organizing, in which the organizers were acting primarily on behalf of

[8] Quoted in Sale, *op. cit.,* p. 132.

[9] See Bob Gottlieb, Dave Gilbert, and Gerry Tenney, ''Toward a Theory of Social Change in America,'' *New Left Notes,* May 22, 1967. This group had been developing its ideas since 1966 and had been influenced by the writings of the French theorists André Gorz and Serge Mallet.

others, anti-war work was understood, especially for male students, as in their immediate interest, as part of a struggle for freedom not only for the Vietnamese, but also for themselves. This consciousness, tied in with the ideas expressed by Mario Savio of FSM, facilitated an understanding of students as apprentice workers.

SDS president Greg Calvert spelled all this out in a speech at Princeton University in 1967. Revolutionary consciousness, Calvert argued, "is the perception of oneself as unfree, as oppressed—and finally it is the discovery of oneself as one of the oppressed." This, combined with an awareness of the gap between what is historically possible, "what one could be" (given the social potential at the historical moment), and "what is" (the ways in which that potential is frustrated by the existing society) are the bases for a revolutionary understanding and for a movement. New working-class theory was a powerful tool, Calvert said, because it enabled students to understand "their special role" in relation to the present structure of industrial capitalism. "Students," he said, "are the 'trainees' for the new working class and the factory-like multiversities are the institutions that prepare them for their slots in the bureaucratic machinery of corporate capitalism." This meant that SDS "must stop apologizing for being students or for organizing students." Students were a "key group in the creation of the productive forces of the super-technological capitalism." The demand for student control, Calvert went on, is a demand to end student alienation in the same way that demands for worker control were aimed at ending alienation at work. If this were true, Calvert concluded, it "was a mistake to assume that the only radical role that students could play would be as organizers of other classes." Instead, Calvert asserted, students should understand themselves as part of a "broad range of social strata" that included the "old" and the "new" working class, as well as the "under-class" of racial and ethnic minorities—all of whom must move together to revolutionize the United States.[10]

This new working-class theory, as expressed by Calvert, constituted a rejection of bourgeois sociological definitions of class (definitions based on income levels, life-styles, or the kind of work one did).

---

[10] Gregory Calvert, "In White America: Radical Consciousness and Social Change," in Teodori, *op. cit.,* pp. 412–418.

Instead, it returned to the Marxian category of class as a relationship to the process of production, to control of property or the necessity to sell one's labor power. By these standards, college students were understood as apprentice workers, despite their social and material advantages. The change in class position of college students followed from the changed nature of production and social organization in the United States over the previous two decades. Advanced technology meant higher productivity and the need for fewer industrial workers to produce more and more goods. Mass production, in turn, required greatly expanded consumption and new markets, domestic as well as foreign. Whole new industries were needed to create, sustain, and manage demand for new commodities—and to absorb the increasing numbers of surplus workers. Furthermore, the social conditions of modern capitalism, particularly its high degree of integration in the face of continuing inequalities, required new industries of social control. All of these workers—technicians, teachers, advertising people, social workers—are part of a contantly changing working class. They have no independent access to productive (profit-making) property and less and less control over the nature or conditions of their work.

The attempt to understand students as part of a potentially revolutionary, diversified working class was part of a general tendency within the new left that saw the anti-theoretical stance of the movement as increasingly unproductive and dangerous. In early 1966 some of the *Studies on the Left* editors had argued that the new movements were in, or were fast approaching, states of crisis, that "the initial usefulness and success of their anti-ideological stances have worn thin," and that the need was for the development of a socialist movement that would think in terms of a post-industrial socialism.[11] The new working-class theory, to the extent that it placed students within a diverse working class, was a step in that direction. But the anti-theoretical and anti-intellectual currents were too strong in the movement. The new working-class theories did have a brief flowering in 1967 and early 1968, when student antiwar activity allowed people in the movement to understand themselves both as part of the oppressed and as part of a potentially revolutionary

[11] Martin J. Sklar and James Weinstein, "Socialism and the New Left," *Studies on the Left,* vol. 6, no. 2 (March–April 1966), pp. 62–70.

class. But when Eugene McCarthy and Robert Kennedy emerged as opponents of the war and the student peace activists began moving toward them, anti-war activity per se lost its power as a substitute for a revolutionary party. At that point the new working-class groups faded in the face of youth-culture advocates on one side and the Progressive Labor Party, with its narrow working-class syndicalist perspective, on the other.

The cultural revolution, given one of its more ideological formulations in a widely-circulated article by John and Margaret Rowntree, "Youth as a Class," reflected the movement's understanding of itself in terms of its own immediate experience. The idea of youth as a class, which was to the student movement what cultural nationalism was to the black movement, emphasized the ways in which young people were different from and opposed to the rest of society. Popular culture and merchandising for the "youth market" reinforced the idea of cultural revolution within the movement. And after 1968 the idea of youth as a class reinforced the view that all of white America—except the revolutionary youth—was hopelessly corrupt ("white skin privilege") and that the only hope for revolution lay in guerrilla warfare by "third world" peoples.

Even in the absence of these competing pressures, it would have been difficult to translate the newly developing understanding of the working class into coherent politics in 1967. Traditional "Marxism" and pragmatic liberal theory weighed heavily in the balance against such ideas, and the SDS leaders themselves (with the exception of the new working-class tendency) had consciously refused to develop their own socialist politics in opposition to the archaic "Marxism" of the old left. In any case, the success of new left anti-war activity, evidenced in a rapidly growing movement and a seemingly spontaneous development of anti-capitalist consciousness, militated against such a development.

/ Crisis and Disintegration

Although it is clear that by 1966 SDS and the new left in general faced a crisis because it had not developed a coherent politics of its own, the decisive turning point did not occur until 1968. Until then, the absence of a defined socialist politics was not immediately detrimental to the movement because both major parties supported the war policies of a liberal Democratic administration. Anti-war activity thus appeared in itself as opposition to the system as a whole. And, in fact, the anti-war movement was constantly radicalizing tens of thousands of people under the leadership of SDS, various old left sects, and radical peace groups. At the same time, the new wave of militance among northern ghetto blacks, starting with the Watts riot in 1965, found organized expression in the emergence of the Black Panther Party, which in 1968 and 1969 grew rapidly in ghettos throughout the country. With the emergence of the Panthers, a loose alliance between ghetto blacks and the new left formed. These developments led many radicals to argue, especially before 1968, that the peace movement was itself a sufficient substitute for a revolutionary party—and in a narrow sense, and briefly, it was.

For those who depended on the peace movement to continue spontaneously making "radicals" or "revolutionaries," that is, to serve both as an anti-war movement *and* as a revolutionary party, the emergence of Eugene McCarthy and Robert F. Kennedy as anti-war Democrats was a disaster. This was so despite the fact that SDS temporarily benefited from McCarthy's campaign or rather from its failure. Following the 1968 Democratic Party convention, with its naked show of force against McCarthy's supporters, many young McCarthy workers flocked into the radical student movement. But this influx was not part of a process of healthy growth, it was a last and superficial rally that barely served to mask the underlying, and fatal, weakness in SDS.

The problem was that fighting to end the war no longer meant fighting all sectors of the American ruling class. Now substantial corporate interests and liberal politicians, especially in the Kennedy wing of the Democratic Party, also stood for a rapid conclusion of the war. This pointed up the need for a new socialist party, independent of the peace movement (although working with and within it), and the short-sightedness of having seen the peace movement as fulfilling the same function as such a party. But SDS and other radical anti-war groups *had* understood the peace movement to be a substitute for a mass socialist movement, and as a result they were now faced with a dilemma: either to attempt to maintain an anti-imperialist (by which they meant anti-capitalist) peace movement outside of, or opposed to, the liberal peace movement or participate in the larger peace movement and drop the idea that it was in itself revolutionary or radicalizing. To do the first was to isolate the left, since it meant losing the support and involvement of those whose first concern was ending the war. Obviously Kennedy, or even McCarthy, could do more to end the war than a minority section of the peace movement. To do the latter meant either trying to organize a new mass socialist movement virtually out of thin air or abandoning the attempt to build a revolutionary movement until the war ended.

In fact, the new left as a whole did neither—or, rather, it bounced back and forth between both alternatives. And in the meantime, both the Socialist Workers Party and the Progressive Labor Party came into their own. Within the peace movement, the Socialist Workers Party and its Young Socialist Alliance (YSA) assumed the initiative and undermined the strength of SDS and other new left groups. Within SDS, Progressive Labor quickly gained strength and threatened to take control—or at least appeared to be so threatening.

The appeal of the Socialist Workers from 1968 to the end of the war in Vietnam was based on a politics that was virtually identical to the Communist Party's Popular Front strategy. Like the Communists in the CIO, the Socialist Workers in the peace movement served as militant organizers for a liberal anti-war movement, while keeping the question of socialism and revolutionary politics the private property of party members and readers of the party press. The Socialist Workers and YSA members had been active in the anti-war movement at least since 1965, when the committees to end the war in Vietnam were organized. But before 1968 they were a relatively minor force because the contradiction of purpose within the peace movement—between being simply a movement to end the war and being a revolutionary movement—had not emerged. In those first years, the Socialist Workers Party was seen more as an annoyance—an unpleasant, disruptive force—than as a threat. But after 1968 their strategy made it possible for them to work effectively with the mainstream of the peace movement—with the liberal Democrats—even while they maintained their private socialist beliefs. For those who wanted to be part of a publicly revolutionary movement, the Socialist Workers Party had no appeal, but for those who were primarily motivated by a desire to end the war, the Socialist Workers Party became increasingly acceptable, if not attractive.

As the Socialist Workers Party's politics pulled people away from the new left in one direction, the Progressive Labor Party's politics did the same in another. Progressive Labor, although active in SDS since early 1966, had, like the Socialist Workers Party, been relatively unimportant. When Progressive Labor Party members started joining SDS, some SDS leaders were apprehensive. But given SDS's commitment to an open organization, no move was made to exclude them. And for the first year and a half or more, Progressive Labor Party members functioned within SDS without gaining much support for their politics. Progressive Labor's main strategy within the student movement was to work for what it called the worker-student alliance. This was based on the belief that the industrial workers were the key revolutionary force in society.

In 1966 and 1967, when the new working-class theorists were in the leadership of SDS, Progressive Labor stood opposed to them with its ''old'' working-class theory. This tended to narrow and distort what was positive in the new working-class politics—a conception of the working class as changing, as increasingly diversified and stratified. In its place, there came to be debates about which was the *real* working class, which was ''key,'' the new or the old, as if there were two working classes, each sharply different. While Progressive Labor put forward its narrow conception of the working class, the new working-class theorists and followers increasingly responded in kind—as if college-educated workers were the new salvation in place of the old working class of previous socialist movements.

But neither the new nor the old working-class advocates made much headway. Progressive Labor's strength, initially at least, lay elsewhere: in its identification with China, Maoism, and the third world, and in its open (within the left) espousal of Communism, symbolized by its waving of Chairman Mao's little Red Book. Progressive Labor's great virtue during this time was in its constant confrontation of SDS with the need to consider the working class and socialism (Communism) if it were to take itself seriously as a revolutionary movement. But until 1968 Progressive Labor's virtue was its own (and only) reward, because SDS as a whole did not see the need for a revolutionary movement or party outside the peace movement.

When this situation changed as a result of the McCarthy candidacy, the SDS leaders, who had constantly pushed the anti-war movement as a surrogate for a revolutionary (socialist) movement, were left embarrassed and politically bankrupt. Suddenly, in the absence of any other alternative, the Progressive Labor Party looked good to many SDS members, especially to those more committed and thoughtful members. And, ironically, within this situation many of Progressive Labor's weaknesses temporarily served as strengths. Progressive Labor had what the rest of SDS lacked: a tightly knit, well-coordinated organization with a distinct ideological line and a firm identification with the leading international anti-imperialist force, China and Maoism. Also, the Progressive Labor Party shared much with the new left: the idea that violence, or the experience of violence, was in itself radicalizing and a confusion of militance with revolutionary (or socialist) consciousness. For the Progressive Labor Party, as for the Communist Party from which it came, militant economism—which meant militant action around an immediate issue or demand—was a substitute for socialist politics (making the question of socialism vs. capitalism an explicit, public issue). But this confusion was also shared by many within SDS and was inherent in the concept of "radical" politics. Within American liberalism, radicalism had always meant militant interest-group activity, mobilizing masses in behalf of some goal within the system.

This confusion of the form of an action with its political content runs through the history of the left in the United States, but assumed its most ideological form in the 1930s, when style, rhetoric, and the degree of personal commitment and self-sacrifice became the only visible distinction between Communists (those who personally felt or understood the need for socialism) and other organizers or activists in the trade unions and other social movements. In the 1930s and 1940s, these militants and their supporters were identified by the left as "progressives." The use of the term radical, which became popular with the new left, was a step toward an open socialist politics, because to some people "radical" meant getting to the root of the problem, which implied an anti-capitalist perspective. But radical was also a term long associated with the politics of the bourgeois revolution, and it was used, often self-consciously, to avoid clarity.

Progressive Labor's conception of the working class also reinforced the new left's idea of itself as "middle class" people whose only legitimate role was helping to organize the truly oppressed. Progressive

Labor's insistence on seeing capitalist society as class society, and the working class as the revolutionary force, was a step forward, but the way it understood this was consistent with SDS and SNCC ideology. Thus, for example, those in SNCC who thought of themselves as revolutionaries believed that building a "lasting mass organization of the poor" to seek power would be "revolutionary" if it could free itself from the "northern, middle-class, interracial element." In this view, it was necessary for SNCC to "choose between reform or revolution, violence or nonviolence," because a revolutionary organization could not "afford weak and vacillating leadership" or "liberalistic *forms* of self-assertion." [12]

This confusion of form with political content, of militant tactics with mass consciousness of the need for socialism, was widely shared within both the black and white sectors of the new left. It became the hallmark of the "anti-imperialist" movement that developed after 1968. Thus, as late as 1971, when the "anti-imperialists" organized a separate demonstration at the time of a mass march on Washington led by the Socialist Workers Party, many radicals understood their demonstration to be "radical" or revolutionary even though the political content of it varied only slightly from the mass march. The distinguishing feature of the Mayday Tribe (the radicals) was their commitment to civil disobedience and to raising issues other than the war itself (multi-issues). Participants in the Mayday demonstrations saw the Socialist Workers demonstration (a march of several hundred thousand people) as "passive and meaningless," while the Socialist Workers undoubtedly thought of the Mayday actions as sectarian and isolated. But neither demonstration appeared to be revolutionary even to an observer as astute as Noam Chomsky. He noticed no participants in the Mayday actions "so misguided as to consider Mayday a step toward overthrowing 'bourgeois society' " and argued that the two were complementary means of applying pressure to end the war, which no doubt was true. [13]

Meanwhile, within SDS, the threat posed by Progressive Labor in

[12] Forman, *op. cit.*, pp. 412–413. Emphasis added.

[13] Michael Lerner, "Mayday: Anatomy of the Movement," *Ramparts,* July 1971, p. 24; Noam Chomsky in *The New York Review of Books,* p. 24. For a fuller discussion of this see: "The Anti-War Movement," *Socialist Revolution,* No. 7 (vol. II, no. 1), pp. 76–78.

1968 began the process that led to the split-up and disintegration of the student movement of the 1960s. The process that led immediately to the formation of the group that became known as the Weathermen began at the 1968 convention of SDS as a coordinated attempt to prevent Progressive Labor from gaining control of the national office or even a substantial representation in it. The strategy of this group, then known as the national office collective, was two-sided. To the majority of SDS members it presented itself as the only practical means to prevent capture by Progressive Labor. To the militants, it presented itself as more revolutionary than Progressive Labor—as the "real" Communists. In its former role it could count on the support of almost all of SDS, but in gaining that support and in working to rid SDS of Progressive Labor, the national collective also laid the basis for the destruction of SDS as a whole and for the splintering of the new left.

One part of the attempt to outmaneuver Progressive Labor was put forward by Mike Klonsky, SDS national secretary in 1968–69. Klonsky combined Progressive Labor's emphasis on the working class with an identification more compatible to most SDSers: revolutionary youth. This Revolutionary Youth Movement (RYM) strategy had the virtue of moving to co-opt Progressive Labor while retaining a unique key group as revolutionary agent. As Klonsky explained it, the notion that SDS had to remain "simply 'an anti-imperialist student organization' " was no longer viable. The nature of the struggle was such "that it necessitates an organization that is made up of youth and not just students, and that these youth become class conscious." This meant that SDS's "struggles must be integrated into the struggles of working people." Organizing young working people into a "class-conscious anti-capitalist movement" would "(a) strengthen the anti-capitalist movement among the work force, (b) provide an organic link between the student movement and the movement of working people, and (c) add to the effect that we will have as a critical force on older working people today." [14] This RYM strategy was similar enough to Progressive Labor's Worker–Student Alliance to appeal to many of the same students, but differed enough to appeal also to many youth-culture adherents. In itself, the RYM approach probably would not have sufficed to head off

---

[14] Quoted in Sale, *op. cit.,* p. 507.

Progressive Labor, but just in time Progressive Labor lent a helping hand in its own demise by condemning black nationalism as reactionary and by specifically condemning black student groups and the Black Panthers.

This happened just as the national office collective was leavening Klonsky's RYM proposal with militant anti-imperialism and identification with the Panthers. Largely at the initiative of SDS interorganization secretary Bernardine Dohrn, SDS developed close relations with the Panthers in Chicago. Illinois Panther leader Fred Hampton (later murdered by the Chicago police) worked closely with SDS. "They help us out in many ways," said Hampton, "and we try to help them out in as many ways as we can." In March 1969 at the SDS National Council meeting, the Black Panthers were recognized as "the vanguard force" in the black liberation movement, and SDS pledged support in the form of money and propaganda for Panther leaders then being jailed and brought to trial in many cities.

The identification of revolutionary youth as the key force among whites and identification with the Panthers and the revolutionary nationalist movements in Cuba, Vietnam, and other "third world" countries served to distinguish the RYM people from Progressive Labor and was a sufficient basis of unity, while Progressive Labor remained as the major threat, which was until the June 1969 convention of SDS. And since most SDS members were strongly opposed to Progressive Labor, the RYM group was able to gain general support as the only means of ridding SDS of the threat of take-over by what was viewed as an alien old left organization.

The Last Roundup

The first noteworthy thing about the 1969 SDS convention, which took place in the old Chicago Coliseum, was the relative absence of the old-time national and regional leadership and of independent rank and file delegates. This was a convention of organized factions, with Progressive Labor and its Worker–Student Alliance having some two-fifths of the delegates, RYM (including what came to be known as the Weathermen and RYM II) having close to that, and the remainder divided among the International Socialist Club (a neo-Trotskyist group), various ill-defined groups, such as Rank and File Upsurge and the Revolutionary Socialist Caucus, and a sprinkling of unaffiliated (and confused) delegates. From beginning to end the convention was a struggle for power among highly ideological, disciplined groups, more reminiscent of the old left struggles of the 1920s than of recent SDS conventions. The last thing that was wanted by Progressive Labor, RYM I, or RYM II was a serious open discussion of any question. "Theoretical" positions were put forth by each group solely for the purpose of rallying its respective supporters. Mystification and ritual language, rather than an open seeking for political clarity, were the order of the day. This appeared to be somewhat less true for Progressive Labor, since it was the aggrieved party with a near majority and could therefore defend established democratic procedure with apparent sincerity. But Progressive Labor was just as capable as others of using political issues as bludgeons rather than as opportunities for political development and education. The use of the new women's liberation movement to attack the Panthers made this clear. When a Panther spokesman put forward his idea of "pussy power" (that women should withhold sex from men who were not sufficiently revolutionary) and then defended that notion, Progressive Labor mobilized the overwhelmingly negative response into a ritual chant—only one of many during the convention—to "fight male chauvinism." This blunder by the Panthers handed Progressive Labor an ideological club for its counterattack against Panther condemnation. The Panthers found it necessary to retreat in the face of the response, but they returned later with a pronouncement from Bobby Seale stating baldly that any movement that included the Panthers had no room for Progressive Labor. In the context of RYM and Weatherman "theory" such a statement made a split mandatory. On this pretext, the leaders of Weatherman and RYM II organized a walkout from the main convention. They were followed by over half the delegates, who assembled in an adjoining hall and proceeded as if they had expelled Progressive Labor from SDS.

For this convention, the Weatherman group had assembled a lengthy statement of principles that combined many of the lessons that student activists had learned through participation in the new left and the anti-war movement with a rationale for the practice that one tendency had developed since the student strike at Columbia in 1968. This document, titled "You Don't Need a Weatherman to Know Which Way the Wind Blows," was written as a way of attacking Progressive Labor from the "left," but it also served to sharply distinguish the Weatherman group from Klonsky's group, now known as RYM II. The Weatherman statement was in essence a document of despair and frustration. The most positive aspect of the Weatherman statement was its repeated insistence that in the United States, the most developed of capitalist nations, monopoly capitalism could be replaced only by socialism and that an intermediate stage of "new democracy" is meaningless in this situation. Similarly, Weatherman argued, for blacks the struggle for self-determination must embody the struggle for socialism.[15] In addition, Weatherman partly distinguished itself from RYM II in its theory of the working class, put forward by Jim Mellen in *New Left Notes* (the SDS newspaper) in May 1969. Mellen argued that Marx's prediction a hundred years earlier that capitalism would produce an increasing polarization between an ever-smaller capitalist class and an ever-larger working class "has nearly come true," that "the complete socialization of production and the concentration of production into the private ownership of a tiny number of people" has almost been achieved. This meant that "the vast majority of the people in this country, who own no means of production and are forced to sell their labor power to someone who does, are members of the working class." At the same time, Mellen recognized that there were "vast differences among working people in terms of wages, working conditions, and relative control over the work process." [16]

But Mellen's concept of increasing and diversified proletarianization ran counter to Weatherman's main thrust, which was that imperialism was *the* issue. In practice this meant accepting the common bourgeois notion of smugly self-satisfied white Americans surrounded by masses of blacks and colonials seeking to redistribute the whites' personal possessions. This view depends on the idea that human beings, narrowly understood as consumers, act only on the basis of immediate economic self-interest—an idea that diverts attention from the people's role as producers and that therefore tends further to divide various sectors of working people.

The Weathermen accepted this view of human purpose partly

[15] See "You Don't Need a Weatherman . . ." in Harold Jacobs, ed., *Weatherman* (Berkeley, 1970), especially pp. 58–59.

[16] Jim Mellen, "More on the Youth Movement," *New Left Notes,* May 13, 1969, reprinted in Jacobs, *ibid.,* pp. 39 ff.

because it explained their own isolation and justified their elitist politics, but also because they never sought to explain their own transformation from "privileged," "middle-class" students into revolutionaries but saw that process as simply a quirk. They did not understand themselves as the products of a massive social transformation that had converted college-educated labor from a narrow elite—as college students had been in pre-World War II days—into a substantial, technically and administratively skilled sector of the corporate work force. They bypassed their own history and development in order to become rootless, detached shock troops for other people's revolutionary movements. Without a historical and class understanding of themselves they were left with only a moralistic explanation of their actions. And as a result, guilt became—and remained—their main lever for moving themselves and others.

In any case, the main thrust of Weatherman theory and practice was to abandon as unprincipled any attempt to organize a socialist movement among white Americans. The function of white revolutionaries, as they saw it, was simply to support black and other "third world" revolutionaries—to play the role of suicide squads in order to give cover to the black urban guerrillas. In short, the resolution was developed to justify a politics of despair and adventurism. To prove that it was impossible to organize white workers, Weatherman argued that whites were corrupted by what it called "white skin privilege"—a higher income than people in the colonial world—and that this wealth was directly dependent upon the labor and natural resources of the Vietnamese, the Angolans, the Bolivians, and the rest of the peoples of the third world. There was, of course, some truth in that view. Under capitalism, American prosperity is increasingly dependent on imperial control and exploitation of the world market. But that was precisely why a socialist movement among white workers was necessary. As long as people accept the framework of capitalism, they do have an immediate self-interest in continued overseas sales and investment, just as defense industry workers have an immediate interest in continued arms production and auto workers have an immediate self-interest in maximizing the output and sales of automobiles rather than in developing other forms of mass transit. It would only be in the context of understanding how socialism will reorganize production as a whole, how it will establish different guiding principles and priorities that "white skin privilege" could be eradicated among the overwhelming majority of the population. In other words, only an explicitly socialist movement could give American workers a common interest with Vietnamese, Africans, and other colonials in opposing corporate capitalism. Short of such a movement, support for colonial liberation struggles can be based only on sentiment, on feelings of pity or guilt, and on self-repudiation.

In order to justify abandoning the white working class, the Weathermen had to provide a substitute revolutionary agent. Given the history of the new left, and the relationship between SDS and the Panthers during 1968 and early 1969, it was natural that this new vanguard would be the blacks. Just as the Weathermen relied on the Panthers to promote and justify splitting with Progressive Labor (expelling Progressive Labor from SDS was how they saw it), so, in theory, the blacks became the key force in the revolution, to the point where the Weathermen argued that, if necessary, blacks alone could win a revolution within the United States. This theory in turn justified continued isolation and hostility to white workers. If, as the Weathermen argued, blacks could make the revolution alone, then it made as much sense to support the blacks as it did to attempt to build a mass revolutionary movement among whites. Indeed, if urban guerrilla warfare had been the order of the day for blacks, as the Weathermen insisted, then it would have made more sense.

But whether or not it made sense, Bernardine Dohrn and Mark Rudd (a Columbia University student militant) argued for the Weathermen that blacks were the vanguard of the revolution, as they had been of radical forces in the United States throughout its history; that there was not and never had been a liberal black movement because in fact the black movement had always been led by working-class blacks. In contrast, white workers and the white middle class were racist and corrupted by "white skin privilege." Therefore, organizing a mass movement for socialism among whites was not only a waste of time but was "objectively" racist—unless the basis of such a movement was antiracism. The order of the day for SDS, said Mark Rudd in a pathetically revealing slogan, was "two, three, many John Browns."

Unfortunately for Weatherman theorists, black militants were guided by forces other than Weatherman theory, as events quickly demonstrated. Only four weeks after the SDS convention in Chicago, the Black Panther Party held a meeting of its own in Oakland, California. This was a Conference for a United Front Against Fascism, the impetus for which came from the concerted efforts of the Nixon Administration to destroy the Panther organization by encouraging police violence against Panther groups in many cities throughout the country. Instead of calling for urban guerrilla warfare at the Oakland conference, the Panthers did what any group would have done under similar circumstances: It called for a united effort by the left to defend the party. Specifically, it wanted legal and financial aid, support for community control of the police, and other measures designed to stop or slow down the attacks coming from the state.

Not surprisingly, the Panthers expected SDS to support their initiative, given both the help the Panthers had given the Weathermen and RYM II in ridding SDS of Progressive Labor and the stream of statements from Dohrn, Rudd, and others that the Panthers were the leading force of the revolutionary vanguard. But since the Panthers had failed to live up to the image of themselves created by the Weathermen for their own factional purposes, SDS refused to support the Panther program. It was not the first time in relation to the left that blacks had been put forward as the leading force until they took some initiative of their own—until they assumed the lead—only to be repudiated by their rhetorical allies. In anger, the Panthers responded in a style that would soon be all too familiar to the Weathermen. Said David Hilliard, Panther chief of staff: "We'll beat those little sissies, those little schoolboys' ass if they don't try to straighten up their politics. So we want to make it known to SDS that the first motherfucker that gets out of order had better stand in line for some kind of disciplinary actions from the Black Panther Party." [17] In rhetoric, at least, the Panthers and the Weathermen remained closely in tune.

Weatherman and RYM II subordination to the Panthers, however rhetorical and short-lived, was an escape from building a revolutionary movement among white Americans and was, therefore, an escape from revolutionary politics. In that sense, the Weatherman stance was a return to the pattern of ghetto organizing and civil rightism in general.

---

[17] Quoted in Sale, *op. cit.*, p. 590.

The main difference was that in the first instance, when whites were excluded from SNCC projects in the South after 1964 and were forced to look into their own communities for a movement and an understanding of their radicalism, the escalation of the war in Vietnam provided a means to do so. This time, however, the remnants of SDS had nowhere to go but from bad to worse: If the blacks refused to play urban guerrilla warfare, the Weathermen would—and would kick the ass of anyone who stood in the way.

First came plans for the "Days of Rage" in Chicago, October 8, including the great "jail break" out of Chicago high schools (abandoned in Chicago because of a shortage of troops). Then came dress rehearsals in Detroit and Pittsburgh high schools. With the Panthers out of the picture, the rage of the Weatherman women—their alternative to the women's liberation movement—was harnessed by the Weathermen in their guerrilla attacks on the high schools. These attacks achieved what the Weathermen desired: They forced people to take sides. But this time it was the rest of the movement as well as the general public who took sides against the Weathermen. What followed in Chicago on October 8 was two hundred beleaguered Weathermen and women running wild through the streets, demonstrating their fury and the failure of their dream.

Weatherman politics was a politics of frustration, guilt, and despair in the face of the failure of SDS to help build a popular revolutionary movement after 1968. The group's "theory," as expressed in the Weatherman document and in the speeches of Dohrn, Rudd, and others, proved to be only ideological window dressing. This became clear when the theory was shown to be wrong on almost every count. The Weathermen asserted that their strategy of building an elite "liberation army" within the United States was based on rising guerrilla warfare in the ghetto and the rapid spread and growth of anti-imperialist armies in the colonies. But the Panthers made it clear within weeks that they were not engaged in armed struggle as the Weathermen understood it. Similarly, both the Chinese and the Cubans (Weatherman models) were turning inward in 1969 and were concerned primarily with their own economic and political development, while revolutionary movements in Africa, Latin America, and most of Asia were in retreat or were defeated. Even the Vietnamese were indicating a clear desire to end the war with something less than complete victory. If Weatherman actions had been based on their articulated theory, they would have given up their role as shock troops and tried something else. Instead, after the fiascoes in Oakland and Chicago they simply went underground. Within a few short months SDS, an organization with some 50,000 to 100,000 members and close followers, was converted into an invisible band of 200 to 300 people, living in clandestine groups scattered around the country.

All the post-1969 splinters of SDS—the Weathermen, RYM II, the Revolutionary Union, Progressive Labor—based their "politics" on self-repudiation and on the implicit idea of redemption through identification with one or another of the "true" or "key" revolutionary agents—ghetto blacks, youth-culture "freaks," industrial workers, or colonial revolutionaries. And all these splinter groups of necessity repudiated the two major ideas of the early new left that had given it its revolutionary impulse and general direction: (1) that "radicalism" was based on an awareness of one's own oppression and (2) that popular participation in the process of social decision-making (democracy) was central to socialist politics. These two ideas had given the CIO organizing drives of the 1930s their ability to galvanize millions of workers into concerted activity, just as they were the motor behind the drive of southern blacks for equal rights during the 1960s. Similarly, they had moved the new leftists steadily toward an understanding of the working class as diverse and stratified and toward an understanding of the necessity of a socialist revolution in order to realize substantial democracy in place of the formal and empty democracy of corporate capitalism.

But these ideas were rejected as part of the same process that led various groups to identify with elitist "Leninist" revolutionary politics. As the student left moved toward a socialist consciousness it fell back on the existing stock of "revolutionary" ideas: the need for an elite vanguard; a narrow concept of class; an emphasis on military action. At the same time it continued to accept bourgeois sociological categories of thought in understanding people primarily as consumers and in defining the working class, or the potentially revolutionary class, in terms of income levels and life-styles, rather than according to their relationship to the process of production. In short, both the process of events and the failure to develop a theoretical understanding of advanced capitalism combined to produce frustration and an overwhelming sense of crisis. The increasing isolation of the new left despite its early growth, and the ease with which many sectors of society vacillated between the new radicalism and acceptance of liberal anti-war leadership, combined to reinforce the already existing elitist tendency within SDS. The Weatherman group was the result.

Even at its height, the Weathermen numbered only a few hundred, while SDS had had upwards of fifty thousand adherents and many tens of thousands more followers in 1968 and early 1969. But numbers alone are not a true measure of the impact of a political tendency. Within the student and ex-student movement Weatherman ideas predominated during the year following the June 1969 convention. The result was a continued process of breakup and disintegration of the movement, a splintering that briefly reproduced a number of political tendencies from the past or from other social experiences. The Revolutionary Union, the Detroit Organizing Committee, and RYM II adopted Progressive Labor's view of the working class with minor modifications and attempted to ''colonize'' factories or working-class neighborhoods. Other groups took up guerrilla warfare and engaged in clandestine bombings of banks, utilities, and other installations. Along with a few organizations like Venceremos, these groups represent an absurd return in form to the earliest days of the Communist Party. The main difference between these groups, which use China as the Communists have used the Soviet Union, and the Communists is that the Communists persisted in their relationship to the Russians for decades, whereas these new groups have lasted only for months. These post-SDS groups are still a part of the organizational disintegration of the new left rather than the beginning of the reintegration of a new Socialist left.

9/

THE WOMEN'S MOVEMENT

The contradictions within the new left between its espousal of participatory democracy and its elitism accelerated the growth of another social movement: women's liberation. Stirrings of women's consciousness of oppression were apparent before the late 1960s, as evidenced by the publication and large sales of Betty Friedan's *The Feminine Mystique* in 1963. But as a large-scale social movement, women's liberation began largely as a reaction to the treatment of women within the new left, although it rapidly evolved into a movement directed against all forms of women's oppression. That an autonomous women's movement was needed, or even that women were systematically oppressed as women, was at first ridiculed by most new leftists, who were in that sense complete products of the 1950s—the years of the "feminine mystique." Historically, the movement for women's rights dates back to pre-Civil War days. It was concerned with many aspects of relations between the sexes, although ultimately the movement centered almost exclusively on demanding the right to vote. As a substantial social force, the movement ended with the adoption of the suffrage amendment just after World War I.

The old left, particularly the old Socialist Party, responded to the women's movement and strongly supported its political demands, as well as the economic rights of women. Women were active in various aspects of party life, were represented in the leadership bodies, were candidates for public office—Congress, governorships—served as editors of Socialist publications, and, in general, were more fully integrated into the Socialist Party than they were in any other political party or group of that period. Yet within the party, and within the international socialist movement as a whole, criticism of the family or of social relations between men and women within the home and outside, was virtually nonexistent. On the contrary, Socialists put themselves forward as the defenders of the family and Victorian sexual relations and criticized capitalist society for destroying the family and encouraging "immorality." Their campaigns against child labor and low wages were often framed as a defense of the family and the ideal of the man being able to earn enough to keep his wife and children in the home. This reflected the actual feelings of most working-class people, especially the masses of working-class immigrants. And it was clearly preferable to having women and children work and still be responsible for household labor. But the Socialists idealized the Victorian conception of the family as isolated and separate from the economy, from public life, even though this separation was unique to capitalist society, and entailed a fixed division of labor between the sexes. Their defense of the family understood and opposed the effects of increasing proletarianization on family life, but the party had no conception of socialism as a process of reintegration of private and public life and of the necessity of the movement to stand for the end of all invidious or involuntary divisions of labor not only between the working class and the capitalist class, but also between the sexes.

During the 1920s and early 1930s, the Communists paid little attention to women as an organized group—largely because the autonomous women's movement disintegrated after getting the vote in 1920. But the social attitudes of Communists were relatively advanced as a result both of the critiques of the family that were widely discussed in the Soviet Union in these years and because of the changing attitudes about sexual relations in the United States in the 1920s. During the second half of the 1930s, however, Communist attitudes moved backward in response to a return by the Russians to traditional family patterns and also in keeping with the social conservatism of the Depression decade.

Thus, for example, Earl Browder's understanding of a model for a women's program was a woman elected to the city council in Hamtramck, Michigan, as a result of leading a "struggle against the high prices of meat." This was understood as an "outstanding example of achievement among women." To complement this entirely economistic understanding of the "woman question," Browder insisted that "all of the immediate measures proposed by the Communists" were "aimed to protect the home," which required only an adequate income. "It is still true very often," Browder said, "that when poverty walks in through the door love flies out the window. Abolish poverty," he insisted, "and the problem of divorce will largely disappear." [1]

Browder did not represent the only understanding of the woman question within the party, although his views and opposition to separate women's activity and organization prevailed until 1945. In 1936, the party published *Woman Today,* which had a nationwide circulation; Women's Councils were organized throughout the country, and attempts were made to organize a Women's Congress and to write a Woman's Charter (a bill of rights for women). The movement for a Women's Congress collapsed and was abandoned in 1937, following an unsuccessful attempt to organize a national meeting. Agitation for the congress was revived in 1939 and 1940 by Mary Inman and Al Richmond but was opposed and killed by the party leadership. Inman, who published a sometime monthly newsletter called *Facts for Women* from 1942 until the end of the decade, developed the thesis that housework produced surplus value, for which women were paid only indirectly through their husbands' wages. She called for recognition of the work women do in the home, and in 1946 agitated for the organization of a Union of Labor-Power Production Workers (Housewives). [2] Although she apparently had some support among the rank and file party members, especially in California, her efforts did not receive recognition from the party leadership.

After 1945, however, when the party was reestablished, there was a renewal of concern about male supremacy within party ranks, a result of the changed role of women during World War II—when millions of

[1] Earl Browder, *The People's Front* (New York, 1938), pp. 46, 201.
[2] *Facts for Women,* vol. 3, nos. 8–12 (August–December 1945); vol. 4, nos. 1–3 (January–March 1946); vol. 4, nos. 4 and 5 (April–May 1946).

women entered industry and took over a wide range of jobs that previously only men were considered capable of doing—and of a general return to class consciousness and an awareness of a need for a "working-class culture." Within the Communist movement, party members were instructed that women should have equal rights to work and political activity, that housework should be shared, and that traditional "family" relations were in that sense unsocialist. Male supremacist attitudes were denounced and occasionally men were expelled from the party for refusing to treat women as equals or for forcing themselves upon party women. But the struggle against male supremacy within the party conflicted with its emphasis on party members living like "ordinary workers" and also with the Victorian moral standards that prevailed among the rank and file members. The result was that the struggle against male supremacy was taken seriously mostly in the student division of the party, and that as party members aged, married, and went to work their lives became more and more like everyone else's.

In the general population, feminist consciousness reached an all-time low during the 1950s. Women were encouraged to stay at home and out of the wage-labor force. The massive movement to the suburbs increased women's isolation. And the political conservatism of the 1950s discouraged any process of social questioning. The youth who were to become the new left in the 1960s were inculcated during the 1950s with the view of women as mothers, housewives, and sexual objects—or as secretaries and servants. Within the new left, despite the rhetoric of participatory democracy, women were treated no better than in society at large—and in some ways worse, since the defenses that non-movement women had against sexual exploitation were ridiculed.

The women who started the women's liberation movement were not only reacting against the attitudes of their male comrades. They were also responding to their experience in society as a whole and particularly to their futures as college graduates. Women went to college during the 1960s expecting their education to allow them to lead creative and self-determined lives, but found that their desires for careers and meaningful work were not being taken seriously. Women went through the same formal process of education as men but were simultaneously instructed (both formally and informally) that their futures lay in finding a man—to whom they had to subordinate themselves. Thus, although the women's movement began in SDS and other movement groups, it rapidly grew into an autonomous movement to end the systematic oppression of women in all areas of social life, a movement that included many women who had not been part of the new left.

The women's movement emphasized two things in its initial stages. First that the personal experience of oppression was not unique or individual but was common and systematic—part of the social division of labor between the sexes—and that therefore the "personal" was also political. And, second, that every woman had the capacity to discuss and understand the nature of her oppression through participating in a collective effort—the small group. The women's movement has raised the necessity for the elimination of involuntary or invidious divisions of labor between the sexes, between children and adults, and in the left movement. The understanding of the need to break down oppressive social relations in these areas of social life has been a major advance over earlier socialist politics. The stress on social relations by the women's movement has been in sharp contrast to the various movement sects that emerged after 1969 and that reproduced the old left ideas of revolution as consisting simply of changing social relations in industry.

The women's movement quickly went beyond its original membership of organized new left women, although its social base remained college-educated white women. Turning its back on the negative experiences that women had in the new left, the movement concentrated on the problems of women in the larger society. Partly because women were developing new forms and a new analysis, it was natural for them to think of the women's movement as qualitatively different and free from the problems of the left. But the inability of the movement to continue its initial rapid growth and establish stable organizations with a unifying politics brought to the fore the similarities between the women's movement and the new left. The basic similarity has been the inability to develop a politics adequate for making a revolution and ending women's oppression. Women in the women's movement have been hostile to theory for the same reasons that the new left was—most intellectual work in this society is clearly ideological and aimed at maintaining existing social relations, including the oppression of women (and, of course, this work has been done mostly by men). At the same time, little theory has been available for the movement to build on, both because there has been no women's movement for many years and because the new left was anti-intellectual. Theory in the women's movement has come from its analysis of the immediate experience of the women in it. This analysis has expanded the left's understanding, but it has also limited the development of the politics of the women's movement. The focus on the immediate oppression of women by individual men has resulted in a tendency to concentrate on men as the enemy rather than an effort to understand women's oppression as a complex situation within advanced capitalism.

Despite the widespread impact the women's liberation movement has had on popular awareness of women's oppression, the movement as a whole has failed to develop stable organization or to transcend local self-help or social activities. In its first few years thousands of women participated in small groups, whose main purpose was consciousness raising and mutual support. But once that initial purpose was served the groups began breaking up. They were an inappropriate form of organization for political action and often frustrated the impulse toward politics by constantly focusing on personal problems and group social relations.

Initially, the women's movement saw itself as entirely outside of, or even opposed to, the organized socialist movement, largely because socialist parties and groups had traditionally seen "the woman question" as secondary to trade union or political electoral activity, but also because of the social conservatism of much of the socialist movement. Radical feminism grew up in opposition to the socialist movement in much the same way as black cultural nationalism emerged in reaction to the politics and social relations of the white left.

Within the women's movement three tendencies have developed. First, a liberal tendency typified by the National Organization of Women (NOW), which functions essentially as a pressure group within the existing dominant institutions, like the Democratic Party. NOW works around questions of job discrimination, equal pay, promotions for women, women's representation and participation in public affairs and elective office, etc. It is the only section of the women's movement with a stable national organization and a more or less coherent program of activity; but its function is the same as that of any interest group pressure organization and is limited by the prevailing principles of capital accumulation that determine and limit liberal reform. For example, it does not challenge hierarchy, bureaucracy, or elitism; it merely demands equal access for women. It is, therefore, an organization primarily of and for upper strata working women—administrators, semi-professionals, and the like.

The second tendency is radical feminism. This tendency is concerned primarily with social relations outside of work, with "private" life, and particularly with finding alternatives to the existing family structure. Because this tendency is based on opposition to the oppression of women within the family, both its theory and its social impulse is largely anti-male, and radical Lesbianism is its ultimate form of expression. Its social base is the same as that of the new left in general—college-educated women who have remained outside the mainstream of the traditional work of this stratum. As such, radical feminism remains a tendency of a narrow social grouping. The logical extension of radical feminism is Lesbianism, since its theory is that the basic social contradiction is between the sexes. In turn, the emergence of a public Lesbian movement and of gay vanguardism has tended to reinforce the isolation of radical feminism as a political movement.

Finally, a socialist/feminist tendency has developed in the women's movement. This tendency, which has much in common with both NOW and radical feminism, advocates equal opportunity for women but also sees beyond this to the need to end all forms of class divisions and involuntary divisions of labor. It is concerned with "private" social relations but sees these as determined by the overall nature of capitalist society and by the imperatives of the labor market and of class society. The socialist/feminist tendency has found no stable organizational forms. A few socialist/feminist women's unions have been organized, but these have either tended to follow NOW's politics or to slide into radical feminism because there is no existing mixed socialist organization or party with which they have identified or have affiliated.

10/

CONCLUSION AND BEGINNING

With the collapse of the new left in 1969, the United States once again had no organized anti-capitalist movement. Beginning in 1900, the Socialist Party had managed to build a mass movement throughout American society for socialism before it disintegrated after World War I. Then the Communist Party had emerged and during the 1930s played a vital role in building the CIO and in various reform movements of the decade. In the years of its greatest strength and influence, the Communist Party did not attempt to make socialism an issue. In the end, the mass movements it helped create and build were all absorbed by the Democratic Party, while the Communists themselves were isolated and widely discredited. Shortly after the final collapse of the Communists' hegemony on the left, the new left began to emerge, but as a loose alliance of several organizations and groups. Unlike the Communist Party, which privately was unified by its commitment to socialist revolution, the new left never did develop a coherent politics. It showed the potential for a new socialist movement, but it did not become one. Instead, under pressure from the Nixon Administration and from various Maoist and Trotskyist sects, and as a result of its own internal failures, the new left exploded in a spectacular re-creation of the worst aspects of old left sectarianism.

By the early 1970s there was no coherent organized left, but all the conditions that created the earlier lefts remained. Social disintegration, economic insecurity, poverty, inflation, and large-scale unemployment continue in the face of unprecedented prosperity for America's large corporations. Political corruption, clandestine and open repression, and a general collapse of morality and morale plagued the Nixon Administration until its demise in 1974, despite Nixon's overwhelming reelection victory in 1972. Even without an organized left, millions of Americans for the first time have begun to lose faith in the existing social system. So much so, that responsible conservative politicians can warn about a crisis of the regime. For the time being the United States is not blatantly intervening with military force to prevent popular revolutionary movements from succeeding in the colonial world. But it continued to support the Thieu regime in Vietnam in violation of the Paris accords of 1973, and it supplied and encouraged the Chilean army, which overthrew the democratically elected socialist regime of Salvatore Allende. In short, the political basis and the social need for a socialist movement exist today as it has for the last century. It is only a matter of time before a new movement for socialism pulls together and grows as a political force in the United States.

When it does, there is much that can be learned from the experience of the Socialists, the Communists, and the new left. From the Socialists a new movement can learn the necessity of making the question of socialism vs. capitalism central to all its public activity, of bringing the fight for socialist consciousness into the electoral arena, the trade unions, and other reform activities. From the Communists' experience it can learn the necessity to avoid a narrow, ahistoric identification with other socialist revolutions, especially those that occur in nations with basically different social conditions than those that exist in the United States. Ironically, despite its many accomplishments, the history of the Communist Party provides only negative lessons. Although it took the lead in organizing blacks, identified strongly with the world socialist movement, participated consistently in trade union activity, and even ran Communist candidates for office, it did all these things in a way that compromised their positive aspects.

Thus it was necessary for the new left to relearn most of what the Communists had experienced. The anti-war movement again had to make clear the need for solidarity with the international socialist movement, as well as the need for an anti-imperialist perspective. The black movement, starting with the civil rights movement in the late 1950s and carrying through to the experience of the Black Panthers and other revolutionary nationalist groups, had again to make plain the need for a multinational movement, and, along with the women's movement, for autonomous formations within an overall revolutionary movement.

And the new left has made its own, genuinely original contributions. The anti-war movement and the student movement, as the sustained core of new left radicalism, have forced a change in the traditional understanding of college-educated people as middle class and have contributed to an understanding of the working class in the United States as increasingly diversified and stratified. This has pointed up the need for a multisectoral movement. And, finally, the women's movement has made it evident that a new socialist movement in the United States must stand for the elimination of divisions of labor in all spheres of social life, and that both in its organizational form and in its immediate politics, a new socialist movement must begin to embody the principles of the new society it is moving toward.

Such a socialist movement, and a party to organize it and give it direction, are necessary and possible. The key problem in the next few years will be the creation of a new socialist party, organized from its inception to contest for state power—for control of society as a whole—so that the vast majority of the American people can, for the first time, determine their destiny on the basis of social need. A new party will have to correspond to the diversity of the American working class, to the need for autonomous and semi-autonomous groupings within or closely associated with it, and the absence of any one sector whose immediate needs are seen as key to uniting all others. Although at different times particular sectors of the working class will play a leading role in the movement—as students and blacks did in different ways during the 1960s and industrial workers did in the 1930s—no one sector is a strategic shortcut to convincing the majority of Americans about the need for socialism and for a socialist party to take power.

So far the developing socialist movement has largely been a movement of college-educated working people and students, ghetto blacks and other oppressed national groups, and women from the same sectors.

Since the decline of the Weathermen and SDS, several groups have organized around the traditional working class—the industrial workers—as the new (or very old) revolutionary vanguard. While their understanding of the relationship of industrial workers to others is wrong, the emphasis has served to correct the anti-worker attitudes of the new left and to point up the absolute necessity to include industrial workers as a substantial, organized part of the new socialist party. To be successful, this new party will have to organize all these groups and others, for example, old people and farmers. But the party will have to be flexible enough to understand, and to try to meet, the needs of every group and to unite them around our common need to overthrow capitalism and to establish a new society. In 1973 and early 1974 several groups were beginning to discuss the possibilities of, and trying to move toward, such a party. The next stage in the development of the left, if it is to move forward and transcend the failures and shortcomings of the past, will be a new socialist party committed to making the need for socialism the major political issue of the 1970s and 1980s.

Index